PRAISE FOR *PARTING WORDS*

'We should all be grateful to this remarkable man, Benjamin Ferencz. This book tells his story with humour, deprecation and real wisdom. To achieve what he has, given the start he had, is the stuff folk tales are made of. How wonderful that sometimes they're true. A lesson for anyone thinking things have never been worse, or can never get better. Bless you, sir'
MARTIN FREEMAN

'I don't know where to stop praising Benny and this amazing book. It must become required reading for every young person looking for a road map on how to live . . . [Ben] is the most inspirational and beautiful person I have had the privilege to read about'
HEATHER MORRIS, author of
The Tattooist of Auschwitz

'Warm, wise and inspiring – a book for our times by one of the world's most remarkable human beings'
PHILIPPE SANDS, author of
East West Street and *The Ratline*

Benjamin Ferencz was born in 1920 in a country that no longer exists. He is a graduate of Harvard Law School and was awarded their medal of freedom in 2014 (the previous recipient had been Nelson Mandela). He was a prosecutor at the Nuremberg Trials in 1947, led efforts to return property to Holocaust survivors after the war, participated in reparations negotiations between Israel and West Germany, and was essential in the establishment of the International Criminal Court. He has four children by his wife Gertrude, who was his high school sweetheart and who sadly passed away in 2019.

Parting Words

9 LESSONS FOR A REMARKABLE LIFE

BENJAMIN FERENCZ

with Nadia Khomami

sphere

SPHERE

First published in Great Britain in 2020 by Sphere

5 7 9 10 8 6

Copyright © Benjamin Ferencz 2020
Written by Nadia Khomami

A CIP catalogue record for this book
is available from the British Library.

ISBN 978-0-7515-7991-8

Typeset in Garamond by M Rules
Printed and bound in Great Britain by
Clays Ltd, Elcograf S.p.A.

Papers used by Sphere are from well-managed forests
and other responsible sources.

Sphere
An imprint of
Little, Brown Book Group
Carmelite House
50 Victoria Embankment
London EC4Y 0DZ

An Hachette UK Company
www.hachette.co.uk

www.littlebrown.co.uk

*To my dear departed wife Gertrude,
who left us on September 14, 2019 after
74 years of happy marriage with never
a quarrel in our loving partnership.*

Contents

Introduction

I often ask Ben Ferencz why he's in such high spirits.

'If you're crying on the inside, you better be laughing on the outside, kid. No use drowning in your own tears,' he replies.

I've previously imagined history as a sentiment reserved for books and the black-and-white film stills we're shown in school. The images of war, destruction, and regeneration feel a far cry from our daily lives. But the protagonists who helped shape the world aren't always fanciful characters from a bygone age, before good had triumphed over evil.

I first came across Ben through sheer chance. I was flicking through US news channels one evening and saw him in a dispatch. I was a reporter for the *Guardian* in London at the time, and his words piqued my interest. When I looked him up I was surprised to learn of his significance, and the depth of his expertise.

In a video, shot in the main courtroom of the partially restored Palace of Justice in Nuremberg – once the site of annual Nazi rallies – I watched as Ben, the chief prosecutor, a punchy and determined twenty-seven-year-old, his short build concealed behind a tall wooden podium, opened the biggest murder trial in history. The twenty-two members of the *Einsatzgruppen*, Nazi extermination squads responsible for the deaths of more than a million Jews and other minorities, stared back at him from the dock.

I'm not sure why it moved me, but I felt a sudden desire to pick up the phone and call him. Maybe it was because I was the same age as he had been during those trials, more than seventy years ago. Maybe it was because of the nature of the news. From Britain's vote to leave the European Union, to America electing a reality TV personality as its forty-fifth president, and civil wars raging across the Middle East, the global postwar order seemed to be unraveling at a rapid pace. Or maybe it was simply because I had just gone through a bad breakup, and I needed someone to remind me that my personal dramas were irrelevant in the face of greater concerns such as war and terror.

I reached out to Ben, and a phone call was arranged. I admit I expected a solemn and somber character.

But the first thing I noticed about him was how empathetic and charming he was. In his 101st year, he remains astutely witty, and despite the horrors he's witnessed in his life is quick to make jokes.

Within minutes it became clear that he had a knack for inspiring. Our conversation went on to run as an interview in the features section of the *Guardian*. The article got the highest attention span of anything we had published that day; as uncommon as it is in this age, people read straight through to the end of the piece. In five years as a reporter, I had never had more positive feedback on a story. Readers of all ages from around the world contacted me to relay how Ben's words had touched them.

The following chapters are the result of a series of conversations I had with Ben over the course of several months. I could say I continued to talk to him so that more people would have the privilege to hear what he has to say. That would be correct, but on a fundamental level I stayed in touch with Ben for purely selfish reasons: he really is quite endearing and funny, and he gives great advice.

'I feel sad today, Benny,' I'll say to him sometimes.

'My dear,' he'll respond, 'whatever it is, I'm sure you've survived worse.'

*

Ben has an uncanny ability to remember minute details and anecdotes from periods of his life, from the full names of those he encountered to what the weather was like on any given day. When I first proposed the conversations that have developed into this book, it took a while to convince him. 'You can't imagine how busy I really am,' he said. 'I'm so busy I don't have time to figure out how I am the way I am, I don't even have time to die.' We went back and forth like that for a while, him insisting he was tied up, and me insisting that it really wouldn't take long. 'My dear,' he said wryly after forty-five minutes, 'you're going to kill your subject at this rate.'

What has struck me the most during the course of our relationship is that, despite an ocean and seven decades between us, there's a lot Ben and I have in common. We both emigrated at a young age and grew up in tough neighborhoods, caught between cultures and continents. We both taught ourselves languages through friendships and subtitled movies. We were both studious but unable to follow rules and regulations. We were the first in our immediate family to go to university, where we quickly realized that we had to work harder and longer to stay in the race. We both studied law, liked to swim, and found humor in the humorless. We even have the same birthday, though each time I remind him of that fact he warns me, 'Don't go doing anything bad and ruining my birthday, kid.'

In the pictures used for the *Guardian* article, Ben is a jovial figure in blue shorts and braces, bouncing around a residential home in Delray Beach, Florida. Hands on hips, he peers from behind his spectacles, a smile on his lips and the sun behind his head. To the average bystander, he's the nice old man next door, the grandfather you pop in to see on weekends and holidays. Ducks can often be heard quacking in his garden.

But Ben is by no measure an ordinary man. He's been referred to as an 'icon in international criminal justice' by Fatou Bensouda, the chief prosecutor of the International Criminal Court; Alan Dershowitz, the noted lawyer and civil libertarian who has represented O. J. Simpson and President Trump, called him the 'personification of the international do-gooder'; and Barry Avrich, the filmmaker behind Netflix's documentary *Prosecuting Evil* about Ben's legal accomplishments, in which they all appear, said he was one of the most iconic figures of our time.

The chapters that follow cover just some of the things Ben has learned throughout his remarkable life, but I'll try to summarize some of his history here. He received five battle stars from the Pentagon for

surviving every major battle in Europe in the Second
World War. He landed on the beaches of Normandy,
broke through the German defenses on the Maginot
and Siegfried Lines, crossed the Rhine at Remagen,
and took part in the Battle of the Bulge at Bastogne.

After being transferred to the headquarters of
General Patton's Third Army in 1944, Ben was
tasked with setting up a new war crimes branch. He
was present at, or arrived soon after, the liberation
of the concentration camps, including Buchenwald,
Mauthausen, Flossenbürg and Ebensee, in search of
evidence of Nazi wrongdoing to present at trial. Ben
dug up bodies from shallow graves, sometimes with
his bare hands. He witnessed scenes of unadulterated
horror that continue to haunt him to this day.

As the US was embroiled in Vietnam, Ben decided
to withdraw from private practice and devote himself
to promoting peace. He wrote several books outlining
his ideas for an international legal body, which became
essential in the establishment of the International
Criminal Court. He also led efforts to return property
to Holocaust survivors, participating in reparations
negotiations between Israel and West Germany.

Ben's career spans more than seventy years, and
he's witnessed more in his lifetime than most. His
is a classic rags-to-riches story. Born into a Jewish

family in Transylvania, he moved with his family to Hell's Kitchen in New York when he was nine months old, and worked hard to escape conditions of poverty before winning a scholarship to Harvard law school.

For his work he has received a multitude of awards, including the Medal of Freedom from Harvard in 2014. The previous recipient had been Nelson Mandela. He continues to use his position to do good, having donated millions of dollars to the Holocaust museum's genocide prevention center. His ongoing efforts to establish a global legal order for prosecuting genocide, war crimes and crimes against humanity are truly remarkable. 'I don't care about glory, I don't care about legacy, I don't care about money – I'd give it all away,' he says. 'I came into the world as a pauper, I lived most of my early life in poverty, and now I'm giving it all back.'

The guy doesn't rest. One weekend, before he headed to Los Angeles to promote the Netflix documentary, I asked if he wanted to trade lives. 'You're off to sunny Hollywood and I'm in rainy London,' I grumbled. He laughed his usual hearty laugh and told me that he would of course trade in a heartbeat.

'I was on a film promotion tour for the Holocaust Memorial Museum once,' he continued. 'We started in New York, from there I went to Washington, LA,

San Diego, and then Chicago. But I passed out. The next thing I knew, I woke up in a hospital. But I was reassured because there was a big cross on the wall of the small room, and underneath it, it said "the resurrection society of Chicago". And I, being a logical person, assumed that if I was being resurrected, I must have been dead. I stayed there for two weeks.'

Death and dying are constantly at the back of his mind. 'I couldn't be better,' he says whenever I ask. 'Do you know why? Because I'm aware of the alternatives.'

There is no one left alive in the world with Ben's perspective. As the last surviving prosecutor for Nuremberg, he has a slogan for anyone keen to ensure that common sense triumphs over murder: 'Law, not war'. He returns to that slogan in every conversation and anecdote. For this, it's been said that Ben is a de facto conscience of the world, fighting every day for a more just reality. According to his son Donald, even family dinners would start with the question: 'What have you done for mankind today?'

'I'm always conscious of how fortunate I have been,' Ben says. 'I was born in poverty to poor parents. I survived the horrors of war in every major battle. I met a wonderful woman. I raised four kids who are fully educated. And I'm in terrific health. No one could ask for anything more. Every time I leave the house or come into it, I count my blessings for the life I have lived.'

Now as a news editor, I'm faced with negative headlines every day. The world seems to be inching ever closer to devastation. The tide of nationalist sentiment has not waned; leaders of the so-called free world promote unilateralism while surrounding themselves with advisers who bang the drums of war; bloody protest movements rage from Beirut to Hong Kong and Paris. Our societies have become a battleground for escalating culture wars, as a 'them versus us' approach abates any empathy and shuns compromise. This is happening as established economic systems breed inequality and corruption, and autocrats pit minorities against one another while attacking constitutional frameworks and institutions. The values and ideals that were presumed to be a given, such as fairness and generosity, are increasingly at risk. Never before has a voice like Ben's been so necessary.

Regardless, sometimes all this gets in the way, and I'm either too busy or forget to call my friend in the different time zone. 'The missing Nadia,' he teases when I finally get a hold of him. 'Are you just calling to reaffirm the fact that I still recognize you?'

But Ben gets it, because he hasn't switched off from

the news either. He knows that the stakes are high, because he's convinced that the next war will be the last one. He continues to make interventions where he deems it appropriate, most recently writing a letter to *The New York Times* when the US and Iran seemed to be on the brink of conflict. 'The charade goes on,' he says, 'they're still behaving like fools.' He tours schools and college campuses giving motivational speeches to kids, and sifts through the reams of fan mail – or as I like to tease him, love letters – that he receives every day, replying now and again.

There are cynics in the world that will have you believe that human beings are set apart by nature of their birth, race, religion, or creed; that refugees are a threat to a nation's prosperity and culture. All sorts of stories about migrant camps, Channel crossings, and detainment centers act to dehumanize the unknown. Intentionally or not, we internalize these stories and doubt ours or others' ability to shine, or do good. But in Ben I saw something that I had failed to recognize in myself: imagination, diligence, and pride. From him we can take lessons in the resilience of the human spirit, even in the face of the worst adversity. We can learn that no matter where we're from or what we do, we have more in common with one another than we know; and that united we are stronger.

Progress is not immediate, it is slow-moving and complex. Miracles, Ben likes to remind me whenever I'm frustrated, can be performed. Weren't basic things such as the end of colonialism and slavery, the rights of women, the emancipation of sex, and even landing on the moon not inconceivable a few decades ago?

Despite his optimism, these months have been a painful period for my friend. His wife, Gertrude, who he had been with for more than eighty years, died recently. He mentions her often, and how she would have been 100 years old now. Reciting her name, and his ongoing love for her, is one of the only things that makes him cry. But at their heart they are tears of joy, because he shared with his soulmate a passion for making the world a better place and improving the lives of others. They were both strangers in a foreign land, who were keen to prove their worth and worked hard to improve their circumstances.

When I ask Ben what three pieces of advice he would give to young people, he never hesitates before answering. 'That's simple,' he says. 'One: never give up. Two: never give up. Three: never give up.' It's this guidance that I carry with me.

Nadia Khomami

1

On Dreams

YOU DON'T HAVE TO FOLLOW THE CROWD

I was born in a house in a country which no longer exists. Transylvania. My sister was born on the same bed as I was a year earlier. She was a Hungarian. My passport said I was a Romanian. After the First World War, parts of Transylvania were ceded to Romania, a country that gained fame as the home of Count Dracula. It didn't matter that the countries had changed their names; it did matter how they were treating their inhabitants. Since both Hungary and Romania were equally antisemitic, it was very advisable for my parents to leave town and get out of the country – or countries – if they could.

That's how my journey began: in conditions of absolute poverty. The peasant cottage in which I was born had no running water, toilet or electricity. There was only one story and an attic. In order to get water, you had to walk several blocks to a well at the center of town.

As soon as we could move we took a small ship to America. We slept on an open deck in midwinter in 1920. We traveled third class, because there was no fourth class. My father, restless and sleep-deprived, was tempted to throw me overboard when I kept howling with hunger, and it was only the intervention of an uncle traveling with us that saved me.

We passed the Statue of Liberty as we came into New York harbor, though I don't remember this considering I was only nine months old. The immigration officer at Ellis Island asked my parents for my name. Since my parents didn't speak any English and the officer didn't speak any Hungarian, Romanian or Yiddish, they got just about everything wrong, apart from my marriage status. My parents gave my Yiddish name: Berrel. He said, 'Bella?' and looked into the cradle and decided I was four months old. It was only by chance, after I had passed my eighty-fourth birthday, that I became aware I had entered the United States under false pretenses: as a four-month-old baby girl.

So there I was in America. We spent the first days or weeks sharing a crowded space at the Hebrew Immigrant Aid Society (HIAS), which provided shelter for entering immigrants. When I did a lecture for them around forty years later, they were surprised but pleased to hear the building was where I spent my first day in America. My father, a one-eyed shoemaker, searched in vain for paid employment. Despite his vision problems, he boasted of his ability to make a pair of boots from a single piece of cowhide. He had lugged his heavy anvils, hammers and shoemaking tools across the Atlantic. Someone should have warned him that there weren't any cows in New York City, much less customers in the market for boots hand-made by a Transylvanian cobbler.

Unable to speak English, barely literate, homeless and penniless, he was happy when a Jewish landlord offered him a job as a janitor tending apartment houses on 56th Street, in a district known as Hell's Kitchen. We were given permission to live in the subterranean cellar of one of the apartments. That was my first home in the promised land, and where my mind came out of its cocoon. I recall the apartment had been partitioned off from the rest of the cellar. Its wood-burning stove was near the large and deep washtub which doubled up as a bath. We had a celebration when we finally got a galvanized metal bathtub, which we put out in the hall and filled with buckets of hot water. The room in which I slept had no windows at all, and the walls were always wet due to the underground foundation. Other parts of the cellar were frequently occupied by alcoholics or vagrants who took shelter from the cold and slept on beds of old newspapers.

They didn't call it Hell's Kitchen for no reason. It was hell. Situated on the West Side of Manhattan, it was lined with old, walk-up apartments; the sort of New York you see in vintage movies, where smoke rises in plumes behind brownstone tenements, and the streets are filled with workmen and gangs smoking on corners. The highest-density crime area in the nation; a kindergarten of hard knocks which taught me a crucial lesson: live and let live.

We were hungry all the time. My parents, who had been betrothed to each other before they were born, didn't get along at all. I was a tiny but active child who never sat still. I cried in a Hungarian accent. My sister and I weren't allowed out in the streets with the 'bums' because it wasn't safe. We would get some fresh air by sitting on the top step of our cellar on the sidewalk level. When my mother went downstairs to cook, I would run away for an adventurous tour. I never felt like an outsider. I was always an American. I knew I was Jewish, but I didn't know I was Romanian or Hungarian. Kids can always understand each other;

we didn't have to speak each other's language. I spoke in a broken way, gesticulating or using whatever words I had, and eventually I caught on.

It's a universal trait in all children. They don't naturally look for differences in their peers in terms of race, color or creed, and they rarely resent their situation until they are told to because they don't know any different. More important than looking for division or having the material things or opportunities unbeknown to them, is a sense of community, fun, freedom, and independence. **It's a state of mind we as adults should try to preserve.**

The residents of Hell's Kitchen were mainly Irish and Italian immigrants, and their offspring seemed primarily intent on beating each other up or playing craps on the sidewalk. I was adopted as a mascot by both sides. In those days there were no distractions such as television, video games or cell phones; the only entertainment was to hang out on stoops looking for trouble.

With so much fighting going on in the neighborhood, crime was considered the normal way of life. My experience as a criminal was limited to pilfering potatoes from a fruit store for cookouts, or being the lookout when my buddies were engaged in some activity of doubtful legality. If a group of kids were ever seen to be kneeling on the pavement, you better bet it wasn't in prayer. They were undoubtedly throwing dice. The kids would put money in a pot and I would protect them from predators or the police. I would stand near a corner and shout, 'Chicky, chicky!' – a colloquialism to indicate the cops were coming. The Irish cop would curse and chase the kids before returning to pick up the pot for himself. I figured if it was good enough for the cops it was good enough for me, so before he doubled back I'd quietly pocket the pennies. I always left something for him, though. Call it a five-year-old's sense of justice.

I wasn't drawing conclusions. I was living one day to the next. **I was living by my wits. Sometimes in life, that's what we all have to do.** When I noticed a number of boys peddling newspapers on Eighth Avenue, I thought I could do the same and make an extra couple of pennies. I assembled bundles of old newspapers I'd gathered from the cellar and began to parade up the avenue hollering, 'Getcher papers!' I did well selling them for two cents, until one day a gentleman looked at the date and realized his new purchase wasn't new at all. He escorted me to my father, who chastised me – before asking, 'Where's the money?'

But money isn't everything. When a young artist was looking for a small girl to model for a drawing for the cover of a popular magazine, my long blond hair – cut in the usual flowerpot style by my mother – and the girl's blouse I borrowed from my sister for the audition, landed me the position. I was paid two dollars and fifty cents, but more importantly, pretty models in the studio would gush over my cuteness and further reward me with hugs and kisses.

A great deal can be accomplished without wealth. My connection with Tony the shoeshine man was mutually beneficial. I would always stop by his little booth, sandwiched between two tall buildings on 56th Street, to bid him good morning. I was learning how to speak with an Italian accent, and he always gave me a Tootsie Roll as a gesture of friendship. If I was ever late, I would take a Tootsie Roll home to appease my mom. Throughout the rest of her life, whenever I tried to sweet-talk her, she would say, 'Here comes Benny with his Tootsie Roll.'

By that point my father, then known locally as 'Joe the Janitor', had become a bootlegger, a position not uncommon in 1920s Hell's Kitchen. At a time when the manufacture, sale, or consumption of alcoholic beverages was against the law, he made whiskey by converting a mash of boiling potatoes in a copper distillery hidden in our basement. My father would give a flask to visitors, including the Irish cops who stopped by for a little refreshment, and the honest ones would leave a couple of dollars on the table. I knew it was murky, so I began speaking openly about Pa's new vocation and friendship with other cops. In what may have been my first victory over organized crime, the distillery soon disappeared.

My interest in crime prevention came from the whole atmosphere in which I was raised. In those days, the movie house on Ninth Avenue became my babysitter. Admission cost only a dime, and my parents would leave me there and pick me up hours later. All the films were the same: the cowboys were the guys with the good hats and the Indians were the guys with the feathers, and the guys with the good hats always won and killed the other guys. But there was also one particular motion picture, a James Cagney film called *Angels With Dirty Faces*, which stayed with me.

Cagney and his friend in their youth attempt to rob a railroad car. His friend escapes and goes on to become a priest, while Cagney is caught by the police, sent to reform school, and later becomes the leader of a gang. He eventually commits a murder, and his friend the priest says to him: 'Look, everybody looks to you, tell them it's the wrong path.' So on the way to the electric chair Cagney starts begging and screaming for mercy. He says, 'I don't wanna go, I don't wanna die,' and then he's executed. The rest of the gang read in the newspapers of how Cagney 'turned yellow' in the face of death. And the question for the viewer is: was he doing it to please his friend, or was he really repentant?

I remember that movie. I asked myself, why is one a law-abiding priest and the other one is a thug? What causes that? I followed that theme, that problem, through much of my career. You might be familiar with the nature versus nurture debate. It explores the extent to which aspects of an individual's behavior are either inherited (the result of genetics) or acquired (learned from the external environment). My conclusion was that our personalities are due to a combination of many things, including the people we surround ourselves with, the opportunities we're given, as well as our self-belief and determination.

My upbringing provided me with early lessons in survival. But I also learned that there are two kinds of folk: crooks and honest people. I didn't think I wanted to be a crook. It was too much trouble. Being chased by the cops, ending up in jail, getting into fights all the time. I learned at a very early age that crime doesn't pay.

There are a lot of places on the planet that are still reminiscent of my childhood neighborhood; perhaps some of you reading this grew up in them. **Whatever situation you come from, believe that you can do something different if you want to.** I am living proof that you don't have to follow the crowd. In America, as in many other places, there remains a big wealth-class divide. A recent study found that 77 percent of those awarded bachelor's degrees in the US come from higher-income families. It is difficult and unfair to go against the grain when your environment is working against you, but it's not impossible. People have pushed against the tide and succeeded throughout history. If someone else has done it, why can't you? Heck, even if somebody hasn't done it, why couldn't you be the first?

My parents were just two of twelve million people who emigrated to America via Ellis Island; they moved thousands of miles to a place where they didn't speak the language, had no friends, no money, no home, and no job. It is perhaps easier to take a leap of faith when you have nothing, but it shouldn't be. This is the first and foremost lesson. If you have a dream, whether it's to change your career, to found a charity, to get fit, to apply for a new job, or to climb a mountain, don't let the fact that your peers haven't done it, or that there are obstacles in your way, hold you back. Man walked on the moon. With the right level of faith and commitment, you can achieve anything you want to.

2

On Education

LEARN WHERE YOU ARE

When I was six my father tried to enroll me in a public school in Manhattan, but they wouldn't take me, noting my unusually small size and the fact that I didn't speak English, only Yiddish. They said come back next year, and the next year they said the same thing. So I was eight years old by the time I started school. It was a school in Brooklyn, and I don't remember learning anything there, other than how to secretly slip buttons off the lapels of the other kids.

Because I started late, I skipped a lot of classes. From grade one I went to three, from three I went to five. I was rotating between my father and mother, so I was also moving schools. My parents had finally decided to get divorced after ten years of unholy acrimony, married new partners and after that they lived happily ever after. **It's important to work out what's**

worth fighting for and what isn't, and sometimes it's better for you if you extricate yourself from a situation incapable of improvement.

Both my parents moved around as often as possible. In those days there was a system whereby landlords with empty houses would give you a one-month concession if you moved in, so my parents would move in, and just as quickly move out, before the month was up. This meant I never stayed at one school long enough to make real friends. I loved to read, and my public library card was well used. My size prevented my participation in popular sports such as basketball, football, or even baseball. I couldn't join the Boy Scouts because my mother thought it was a military organization. I was very much a loner throughout my adolescence. **Friends are important but it's good to make peace with your own company,** and I suppose this helped me to know my own mind and trust my own judgment.

Right after the divorce, my sister and I temporarily moved in with an aunt in Brooklyn. She would take me to nearby Coney Island, and I have memories of screaming as she dunked me underwater, the waves crashing overhead. One Sunday, you could barely see the sand on the beach for all the blankets. My aunt left me on a blanket and told me she'd be right back.

I gave her a long period of time – maybe four minutes – and started to frantically look for her until I was intercepted by a cop. I told him, in my typical honesty, that my aunt had gotten herself lost. He took me to the police station and put police caps on my head, as the loudspeaker boomed, 'Tante Fani, Tante Fani, little Benny is looking for you. Fani, please show up.' When my aunt appeared, instead of jumping for joy the first thing she did was slap me around the face. Some people are really ungrateful.

So if I wasn't smart, I was a Smart Alec, often entertaining myself. In a vocabulary lesson in a school in the Bronx, when I was nine or ten, we discovered the word 'harass'. I pronounced it 'haar-as'. The teacher said no, 'har-ass'. I said, 'Her ass?' and rolled around the floor laughing.

When I was promoted to the eighth grade, I was invited to star in the graduation play. The play centered on a powerful but grumpy king who always complained about his troubles and pains. His doctors concluded that the only remedy was to wear the shirt of a happy man, so the king's guards scoured the entire kingdom but failed to find a single person who didn't have some sad tale to tell.

By chance, while wandering over a meadow, the guards heard the merry sound of a flute being played by a young shepherd: me. When asked if he was happy, the puzzled boy said he found joy in every day.

'Quick,' said the guards, 'you must give us your shirt to save the life of our sovereign.'

'But,' replied the boy, 'I do not have a shirt on my back.'

When the apprehensive messengers, fearing the king's wrath, reported back that the only happy person they could find in the kingdom did not even own a shirt, the monarch roared with laughter.

I have tried to live up to the role of the merry shepherd ever since. **Happiness doesn't always derive from the material.** I am an example of that. I have witnessed real nightmares in my life, but they have never detracted from my sense of optimism or gratefulness.

Long-term happiness comes from fulfillment, which will look different to all of us. It might be having a grand purpose, like saving the world. It might be a vow to be kinder to those around you. Or it might be setting yourself tiny goals, like going for a walk, doing your homework, or picking up the dry cleaning – that you can tick off as achieved each day.

The biggest impediment to fulfillment is comparison. Horses wear blinkers to stop them from seeing what is happening around them; this keeps them calm. Sometimes we need to wear blinkers too. Don't let others' achievements prevent you from feeling pleasure at your own, and always remember that someone else's joy doesn't snuff out yours, either.

Finding a little bit of joy in every day of your life will sustain you; it will be the little bit of fuel added to the hearth that will keep your fire burning. Telling yourself that when you have your dream job, or dream house, or dream partner – mystical goals for a future you haven't yet reached – you will be happy is more likely to make you low-level miserable. To find joy, you must look for it around you. Happiness doesn't owe you anything. It is not a person or an establishment to rage against. It is an emotion, and you are in charge of your emotions. You can choose where to find joy. How blue the sky is today, how nice it is to have a full lunch, or be tucked up in bed when a storm rages outside, to have a particularly good cup of coffee. You must look for the happiness in things to be able to find it and feel it.

I have always had a very peculiar mind. If I heard something once, I knew it. One day, during a period in which I was living with my mother and stepfather in the Bronx, my eighth grade teacher, Mrs. Connelly, asked me to bring my parents in for a meeting with the principal. I thought, what have I done now? Mrs. Connelly explained to my mother that I was an unusual child, a fact she no doubt already suspected. But much to her surprise, the teacher wanted to talk about sending me to a special school, not for juvenile delinquents but for 'gifted boys'. Neither my mother nor I knew what they were talking about – we weren't in the habit of receiving gifts.

Mrs. Connelly explained that there was a special high school in New York called Townsend Harris, one of a kind in the country, where if you pass all the courses it would ensure automatic admittance to the College of the City of New York, without any tuition charges. We didn't know anybody who went to college; to finish high school was regarded as the highest possible academic achievement for immigrants like us. Suddenly I was interested. A new door opened new opportunities.

The teachers at Townsend Harris were college professors, the courses geared to college students. I learned a very important lesson: that you had to study. I'd never studied before. I promptly flunked French and algebra. I only became interested in French when I fell in love with a beautiful French girl called Danielle Darrieux. She was an Ingrid Bergman-type movie star whose films were shown in the nearby arts theater. She would be wooed by Charles Boyer. I kept one eye on her and one on the English subtitles. That was a wonderful teaching tool, and while I came out sounding like Charles Boyer, it made my French professor's explanation of the Battle of the Marne more tolerable. I went on to become a valued interpreter, and after the war even translated for René Cassin, the French Nobel Prize-winning author of the Universal Declaration of Human Rights, who was on tour in the United States. All from falling in love with a French girl. But she was beautiful.

It's a lesson for all of us that you can learn where you are. When you watch a film, read a book, walk along a street, have a conversation – don't be passive about it. **Everything you do is an opportunity to learn something new**, and you never know when that knowledge will come in handy.

In high school I had no money to eat lunch, so I devised a method to get funds by buying a punch card with a hundred holes, putting a rolled-up piece of paper that contained either a fortune or prize in each hole, and charging kids a penny to play. Winnings ranged from one to ten cents. It was a business venture that would have made my Hell's Kitchen gang proud. But the janitor complained about the pieces of scrap paper lying around the locker room. I was summoned to the office of the dean, a bully named Mr. Chastney, who demanded to see my father lest I be expelled. I hadn't seen my father for a year, but I ran to the phone and pleaded with him to come to the rescue, explaining that I was in danger of being expelled.

'What means expelled?' he asked.

I explained it was a bit like being shot.

'For what?'

I said I had been trying to earn my lunch money.

'For this they want to shoot you?'

So my father came in to receive a lecture on gambling, and how fathers should train their children, and how I would have one last chance, and God bless America! My bewildered father followed my instruction, which was to say nothing and just nod.

But Mr. Chastney, the strict disciplinarian, didn't much warm to me after that. He called me in sometime afterward and said I'd been reported for not attending my gym classes. I told him I was an excellent tumbler and could shimmy up a rope faster than a monkey. I was also much sought after as the top man on the human pyramid. 'Every gym teacher knows me,' I said. 'I'm not attending those classes because they happen to be during my lunch hour.'

But the bureaucrat gave me an ultimatum: 'If you don't attend those classes on schedule, you'll not be admitted to City College.'

I thought that was rather harsh. Not being a man to accept such holy baloney, I went to City College the next day and asked to speak to the dean of admissions. He was a jolly Irishman. He said, 'What's your name, big boy?' I said my name was Ferencz. He put his arm around my shoulder and said, 'Well, Terrence, big boy, what can I do for you?' I asked whether I would be admitted to City College from Townsend Harris without passing gym. He said, 'Of course, Terrence, my boy, we'd be glad to have you.' I thanked him and ran off before he could discover I wasn't Irish.

I went back to Mr. Chastney and I said, 'Sir, you lied to me!' He was furious and told me I'd never get a diploma from the school. And so it came to pass that I was admitted to City College without a high school diploma. The lesson should probably be don't endanger your future by winding up the people who have it in their hands, but actually the lesson is: **you don't need to accept something is a truth just because a person in authority tells you it's so.** The greatest geniuses in history became so because they questioned the geniuses who came before them. Some people like to say 'think outside the box', but that is a lot of pressure. The key, actually, is just to think – full stop.

*

City College – 'the poor man's Harvard' – had open admissions, and many students came from immigrant homes. College was an opportunity to share the American dream, not a place for fun and games, and we were deprived of even a football team.

I majored in sociology and social sciences. Distressed by what I saw in Hell's Kitchen, I looked forward to a career that would enable me to prevent juvenile delinquency. I was a good student, but only if I was interested in the subject. In biology I refused to cut open a live frog, so they made me take botany instead, which struck me as a wholly useless endeavor. I almost flunked. It was in Latin as far as I was concerned.

For my philosophy course, I had to read Aldous Huxley's *Ends and Means*. It was from those essays that I came to the conclusion that lawful ends can only be sought by lawful means, earning myself an 'A'.

I got the top grades in all of my social sciences courses. In criminology, when trying to find a solution to the problem of juvenile truancy, I intuitively knew the answer: the kids refused to go to school because the teachers and courses bored them. I was recommended for an unpaid summer job as a counsellor in a reform school in Dobbs Ferry called the Children's Village. It was a classic, modern juvenile detention facility. Every little thug who wouldn't go to school without committing some crime ended up there. I would look after the kids, most of whom had a similar background to me – a bad neighborhood, divorced parents – and it suited my quest to find out why some people become criminals and some don't (the James Cagney dilemma). Plus, it got me out of the hot city in the summertime.

Among other things, I helped build them a swimming pool and teach them to swim. They attached a big diving board to a tree which overhung the pool, and they'd jump in to show how heroic they were even if they couldn't swim. Or they'd try to drown the kid they didn't like, and I'd have to jump in and jab them in the eyes so they would let him go.

The kids had been sentenced there for committing all sorts of crime, from murder down to robbery. Each time I returned from my home in the Bronx, I would bring them back bags of candy, storing them under my pillow for safekeeping until I could distribute them at the optimum time. They promptly disappeared before I had a chance to do this. So I decided to set a trap for the thief. I returned with a box of strong mints and the bait was immediately taken. When I lined up the kids and put my nose under their mouth I smelled the mint right away. I said to the other kids, 'I'll leave it to you to do justice,' and I left them. The other kids beat the culprit up, but the crime was never repeated. Peace and justice go hand in hand.

Recently I received a very interesting document. It was my high school diploma, from Townsend Harris High School. More than eighty years after I left.

The letter from the principal stated:

Dear Mr Ferencz, the date is October 15th, 2019. After reviewing your high school records, at the request of your son Donald, it gives me great pleasure to award you the Townsend Harris High School diploma. This shows that you have completed the high school course of study and have met the requirements of Townsend Harris High School. I congratulate you on this accomplishment and wish you all the best in the future.

I replied, saying:

It gives me great pleasure and a good many laughs to receive from you my high school diploma. I've been waiting patiently for this document for the past eighty-two years.

It will give me great joy to put it on my wall

right under my doctorate of law degree from
Harvard law school in 1943. I can explain that I
am a slow learner.

Three lessons: **patience is a virtue, good things come to those who wait, and, despite the frustrations and resentments, you must take the laughs where you can.**

Were it not for my studies, of course, my life would have been different. I would have become a janitor like my dad, or I would have been one of the kids in the reform school. City College was a college for poor kids. It was a way to make a better living. It was there that I realized the value of education. We can – and should – all learn wherever we are, but the doors institutional education open up for us should not be underestimated. I worked hard and was clever, but I was also very lucky that Townsend Harris and City College existed. **This is a lesson in appreciating our own luck and privileges, and also to remind us that others do not have them.** What will you choose to do about that?

3

On Circumstances

LIFT YOURSELF BY YOUR OWN BOOTSTRAPS

Some uncle of mine, commenting on my behavior, said, 'Benny's going to be either a good crook or a good lawyer.' As I have said, I knew I didn't want to be a crook, so there was only one other option remaining.

I had no idea which was the best law school in the world, but I wanted to attend it, for the very simple reason that being about five feet high, I was often abused by people who were taller in stature. I thought the only way I can compete is by being better than the others. **Your weaknesses can become strengths if you use them to propel you.** Don't complain about adversity; it won't solve the problem so it's a waste of your time, and besides, it is a better teacher than plain sailing.

I didn't know the difference between a law school in Brooklyn and a law school in China. I inquired and was told the best was Harvard, so I applied and was accepted for reasons I'm yet to know. I was about twenty years old. I had no idea what to expect. I remember very well when we had an introductory lecture by the dean. He said, 'Look to the right of you, look to the left of you. At the end of this semester, one of you three will not be here.' They had a trial period, apparently, and the bottom third of the class would automatically be dropped. It made everybody freeze. I was frightened into the possibility that I might not come back, but I stayed and did very well. So well that after my first exam, Criminal Law, I was given a full scholarship for all the time I spent there.

The first thing I learned at Harvard was the meaning of fear. The professor of Property Law, Edward Warren, known as 'Bull' Warren, seemed to have drawn inspiration from the Spanish Inquisition. He would shout out grades at trembling students in the middle of class. One day, he called one poor classmate forward, handed him a dime, and told him to phone home and advise his parents they were wasting their money since he would never become a lawyer. **But fear is only as negative as you let it become;** we experience it because it helps to keep us alive, or – in modern-day workplace or educational situations – achieve the life we want or maintain the one we have become accustomed to. If you are afraid it's because you have something to lose, and that is a good thing. It means you have something to fight for; by concentrating on that instead, you can channel fear into productivity, efficiency, courage, speed – whatever the situation calls for.

Warren taught me the difference between 'personalty' (property that is movable) and 'realty' (real estate), and to never be late. **Being on time – or better yet, early – is one of the easiest successes you can hand yourself,** plus it makes you feel more confident for whatever is about to follow. By not wasting anyone else's time by being late, you're also avoiding antipathy toward you. Practice punctuality: easy wins are still wins.

The Contracts professor, Lon Fuller, taught me that understanding an opponent's point of view is an invaluable skill. For a lawyer it is a way of anticipating an argument so you can defeat it, but it runs true in regular life, too. **It's only by understanding another person's way of thinking that you'll be able to reason with them and perhaps change their mind.** If you have a feud with somebody, then try to understand their perspective: what is it about their background, their current circumstances, their peer group, their personality that has led them to it? Even if understanding their stance won't make them reasonable to understanding yours, it might reduce your anger toward them, and that in itself is a good thing. Anger is not a productive long-term emotion for humans to experience.

The antithesis to hate is to try to change the opinions you don't agree with through compassion, compromise and courage. You begin at the earliest level. When little Johnny is playing baseball with little Tommy and he doesn't like what Tommy does, you teach him he doesn't hit him with a bat, he talks to him and tries to settle it.

The Ethics professor, Zechariah Chafee, taught me about tolerance and **the need to treat all human beings justly**. This doesn't only mean the people who look and sound like you, your countrymen and neighbors, nor does it mean only law-abiding citizens – this means everyone. You are 99 percent genetically identical to every human being on the planet, whatever they look like, wherever they come from, wherever their great-great-great-grandparents came from, whatever language they speak, whatever beliefs they hold, whether they are criminals, evil or psychopaths. It cannot be one rule for them and another for you or for me – under any circumstances – but especially when it comes to justice, which should be the pinnacle of civilization and serves to protect us all. It seems a strange thing to have to stress this in the twenty-first century, but needs must. On an everyday basis, it also means the person down the street you don't like, and your cousin you've fallen out with, and the person you manage at work. 'Justly' is defined by the *Oxford English Dictionary* as 'morally right and fair'. Ask yourself if that is how you treat everyone you speak to or about, and make appropriate changes if you don't. Nasty people can still lead remarkable lives, but in my humble opinion, it doesn't amount to the same.

The most learned scholar of all my teachers, Roscoe Pound (who started his career as a botanist, of all things!), opened my eyes to jurisprudence, and the historical origins of different legal schools of thought. This is an academic lesson that could take up several books – and certainly has – but which you will be glad to note I won't go into here.

Those teachers gave me the confidence to believe that, if I put my mind to it, I could match the best of the best. For one of my most significant lessons from Harvard was the realization that there are different classes of people.

The school was full of rich kids. The students who got up every time they asked a question, and wore argyle socks and brown loafers, and were members of fraternities and drank cocktails, seemed very strange to me. My life at Harvard was a grind as well as an opportunity. While they went punting on the Charles River on the weekend, I lived in an attic, which I shared with a Jewish boy from City College because I couldn't afford the rent of $8 a week alone.

In that attic, I had a small desk with one single light bulb hanging over it. I would look down from my window and see some of the other Harvard boys out having fun, including one who was always polishing his fancy red convertible in the backyard of the neighboring house. I thought, 'I wonder if he knows how lucky he is?' If I wanted to go home on the holidays, I had to hitchhike.

But I had nothing to do with those guys, and they wanted nothing to do with me. I never participated in social outings, like going down to Boston to watch the burlesque show, or having dates with girls. I said to myself, 'Ben, you're wasting your time there.' I was only ever studying or trying to earn enough money to eat. It was my deliberate goal to do the best I could.

Why? Because I had no money. I came from a background where my parents had never read a book. We didn't know anybody who went to college; that was a different world. I knew I had to work harder to get to where I was, because I didn't have a rich father to bail me out of trouble or buy me a fancy car.

I had suddenly found myself in the best law school in the world, and given the chance to lift myself by my own bootstraps. I thought, 'Boy, if you don't give this your best shot, you'll regret it forever.' I wanted to stand out for my knowledge, not my wealth. That's what drove me.

Some people need to feel they have a safety net available if they fail. This makes sense. Knowing that if you're fired from your job, the worst that would happen is you'd have to take out your savings or move in with your family can make you feel less afraid of taking risks and making mistakes. But as a person who did not have a safety net in the earlier part of my life, I can also attest to the virtue of imagining you don't have one. If you were on the side of a mountain, and below you were sharp rocks, and above you was the top of the world, you'd dig deep and find the courage and the strength to climb the mountain. Safety nets can make you lazy. **Needing what you want can make you hungrier, more driven, more creative, more passionate.**

For the duration of my studies, my lack of funds was a constant concern. I had borrowed $500 from my mother when I left home, but that was spent on rent. On Sundays, a hotel opposite the law school featured a special buffet brunch, and for fifty cents I could fill my stomach for a few days. To keep from starving the rest of the week, I found work as a busboy in the cafeteria of the nearby divinity school. In exchange for clearing tables after meals, I could eat my choice of leftovers. I was so grateful that, years later, around 2016, I visited the divinity school and met the new dean there. I was working on world peace, and we had a long chat about that, and we became allies. Then I said, 'Look, I want to pay for my lunches.' I gave him a little envelope and said I would prefer it if we didn't mention this to anybody. Inside was a cheque for $50,000. I share this with you now because one, isn't it a nice story? And two, because I'm a believer in giving back. If somebody helps you out, help them back when you're able to: there's no statute of limitations on that, and you don't have to do it with money. **Gratitude completes you in a different way to anything else.**

During my three years at Harvard, my paradise became the law library. It was there that I found wonderful books and wisdom in the decisions of towering judges like Benjamin Nathan Cardozo, Learned Hand, and Oliver Wendell Holmes. Years later, in my first law office, I hung portraits of all three on the wall above my desk. When a visiting judge remarked that the legal giants looked down on me, I replied that actually, I was looking up to them. **Don't let great men or women daunt you; choose to be inspired instead.**

I had other odd jobs at Harvard, such as coaching some of the other students. I then found a program through the government where if you worked for a professor they gave you a stipend. I originally approached Pound, but he turned me down. I went to see the next professor, Sheldon Glueck. He was the only one teaching Criminology, which was the field I wanted to be in. His first question was, 'How much is it going to cost?' I said it's free, he said I'll take it.

So I became his assistant. And since Glueck was considering writing a book on German aggression and atrocities, my first assignment was to summarize every book in the Harvard library that related to war crimes, a task which probably changed the course of my life. After the war, when the army turned to Glueck because he was consulting with the Pentagon, he told them to find me, and I got the tap.

I never expected to finish law school. When the war broke out, the dean, James Landis, wrote to my draft board asking for an extension so I could finish the semester. He said I had unusual promise. When the term was over, I sent all my books and papers home because I expected the draft to call me up any day. But they didn't. My mom said, 'Ben, go back to school – if they need you, they'll call you.'

My studies during the last two years at law school suffered from the anticipation that I would have to leave at any moment. My notebooks became full of scribbles, because I never thought I'd finish. I didn't attend the classes in Taxation, which were mandatory. I didn't buy the books, which were expensive and big. I took the exam and of course I flunked it. Despite that, I was able by the nature of my knowledge of law to get very rich. I've donated millions of dollars to Harvard and to the Holocaust Memorial Museum since. I hope it shows what you can do when you lift yourself up by your own bootstraps.

4

On Life

THE PATH IS ALWAYS BUMPY, NEVER STRAIGHT

I was sitting at my desk in the attic when I heard the radio report that Japan had launched an attack against the United States at Pearl Harbor. Hitler had already conquered most of Europe, and he and his allies had now declared war against America. Every student I met was ready to enlist.

I spent my time trying to get into the military service that I wanted to be in. The Navy was off the cards, because the idea of drowning at sea didn't particularly appeal to me, and I was sure the Marines wouldn't take me because of my size. So I wrote to the war department and suggested I might be most useful in the intelligence services, thanks in part to my language skills in French, Hungarian, Yiddish, German and Spanish. I thought if they dropped me behind German lines in France and taught me how to use dynamite, I could go blow up all their trains and communication lines. I had even figured out in my mind how I would do it: by disguising myself as a nun on a bicycle. I'd wear the garb and have a close shave. But I was told no one could serve in the intelligence services who had not been a US citizen for fifteen years – and I had been a citizen for fourteen years (since my dad applied for his papers). I tried the Air Force, because if you got shot down you at least usually got killed, but they concluded I had to be 5 ft 4 in. to reach the pedals and didn't qualify. Then I applied to be a navigator, but my sense of direction was so terrible that they said, 'Ben, if we told you to bomb Berlin, you'd probably end up in Tokyo.' And when I tried the paratroopers, they said I'd go up instead of going down.

As soon as I graduated from law school, I reported to the draft board in the Bronx. There, the clerk told me he had been a student at Yale law school when the First World War broke out. He became a pilot and lost a leg in combat. He said he never went back to law school and had regretted it ever since. When he had seen the letter from the Harvard dean asking for more time before I was drafted, he decided he would not let happen to me what happened to him. By pure chance this man I'd never met had let me finish law school.

I knew much about Nazi aggression and their plan

for concentration camps because of the research I undertook for Professor Sheldon Glueck. He was part of a group of lawyers from countries that had been occupied by Germany that were already collecting war crimes evidence. So the US Army, in its infinite wisdom, made me a private in the antiaircraft artillery, of which I knew absolutely nothing.

My military career began dismally. I was assigned to be a typist in the 115th triple-A Gun Battalion, but I never did learn how to type or how to fire a cannon. My primary adversary was not the German army but the American army, where it quickly became clear that rank had its privileges. They gave me every possible dirty assignment they could find, including wiping the toilets, cleaning the stinking grease-pits, and scrubbing pots and pans. I had to sweep the floor so many times that by the fifth time I was ready to take that broomstick and use it in ways they had never anticipated.

I went through basic training in Camp Davis, North Carolina. Countless times, when I politely let my army superiors know that I thought a military mandate was particularly stupid, I was screamed at and warned: 'You're not supposed to think!'

We sailed on the HMS *Strathnaver* to England, where the general explained our mission: intercepting low-flying enemy craft that were expected to attack men on the beach. He said we had nothing to fear, because our secret new radar could detect any approaching aircraft, and when the aircraft was within range, our new remote control would automatically shoot it down.

But when the time came, not only did the Germans know exactly what our radar was doing, they used carrier pigeons coated with aluminum paint to blur detection and distract the guns. So we'd all be firing at opposite directions, allowing the target to bomb the hell out of us. I don't know how many German planes were shot down by the 90 mm cannons of the 115th Gun Battalion, but I do know many of the planes hit were British or American. I learned quickly that just because the general tells you it's so, it doesn't mean you should believe him. Another reminder that we must all be capable of thinking for ourselves.

At the southernmost tip of England's foot, at a place called Land's End, our battalion stood by for the long-awaited invasion that never came. I recall instead the early-morning hours of June 6th, 1944 – D-Day. The sky turned black with planes, and all the ships that had been clogging the harbors along the British coast set sail for France. We crossed the Channel, zigzagging to avoid German submarines, and landed on Omaha

Beach, Normandy. I jumped into the water from my landing craft. For most, the water came no higher than their knees; for me it came to my waist. The skies opened up in pouring rain. One British soldier patted me on the back and said, 'Good luck, Berlin is that way.'

I made my way to the top of a ridge where the rest of my outfit was located. I was immediately seized upon by one of my buddies, 'Starchy' North, who was in a large hole manning a .50 caliber machine gun. He said, 'Boy, am I glad to see you,' and told me to take over. He disappeared and came back with a bottle of Calvados, a local brew akin to rocket fuel. Suddenly, Starchy went rigid and fell face first into the sand. I thought he'd been shot in the back by a sniper. But he wasn't dead, he was dead drunk. There in the heat of battle. It wasn't all heroic.

I trailed along with the 115th triple-A Gun Battalion for quite a while. In my three years in the army, I went through the Maginot and Siegfried Lines – which were big walls put up to keep out guys like me (President Trump should take note of the value of walls; I went through both without getting killed even once) – crossed the Rhine at Remagen, and took part in the Battle of the Bulge at Bastogne.

I recall happy scenes, such as dining with a French

family on 'Lunéville Liberation Day', singing French songs and toasting the Allies. I also remember somber days, like the incident at St. Lô, which was a crossroads occupied by the Germans, though we had control of the air. The sky darkened with long waves of our Flying Fortress bombers as they soaked the city below with massive bombs. Standing several kilometers away, I felt the ground shake so fiercely that I couldn't stand. No house or building was left intact. I still wonder how many innocent people were buried under the piles of rubble.

I faced all kinds of dangers, but I can't say I was ever frightened. I just dealt with it. They called me 'Fearless Ferencz'. I don't know where that came from. I don't think I'm a very heroic type of guy. But from a young age I learned to defend myself. If somebody challenged me, I would kick him in the balls and then kick him in the head with my knee as he went down. At a very early age I was accustomed to bullies. They never bullied me twice. War was the same. **Don't let anyone bully *you* twice.** Stand up for yourself.

My first sergeant was a mean son of a bitch from Texas who boasted about how he beat up his wife regularly. If I had a choice of killing him or Göring I would have shot him first. He said, 'You wanna become an officer?' And he took my application, which had been approved, and threw it in the trash can, saying, 'The only way you'll get out of this outfit, soldier, is in a box.'

That summed up my membership of a combat unit, where it seemed to me the object of the soldiers around me was to make my life miserable. It was me versus the US Army, which once even threatened to have me executed for cooking a chicken. You'll no doubt be wondering why. Well, the French were so grateful to be liberated from German occupation that they cried, cheered, and raced after the vehicles handing out flowers, wine and eggs. Since we were all living on army spam, an inedible mixture designed to kill people, we were very happy for the eggs. But soon, a sign was put up on the trees: 'INDIVIDUAL COOKING IS NOT ALLOWED, BY ORDER OF THE COMMANDING OFFICER'. The colonel didn't like the area being strewn with eggshells.

I couldn't believe he wouldn't let the guys eat an egg, so I exercised my constitutional right to life, liberty, and the pursuit of happiness by inviting three of my enlisted friends to a chicken dinner. But we were quickly made to report to the colonel for disregarding orders. He asked me if I knew what it meant to disobey an order in a time of war, and told me he was going to make an example out of me. I thought this son of a bitch is going to have me shot. I said, 'Sir, I wouldn't do that if I were you. Your order said no individual cooking, I wouldn't disobey that. I have three witnesses that can testify it was group cooking.' He turned red, white, and blue, a patriotic man, and screamed for me to get out of there.

A couple of weeks later there was a list of everybody in the battalion who were receiving good conduct medals – about fifteen hundred names. Only one name was struck out with red ink: mine. I went to my captain and said to what can I attribute this dishonor? He said, 'You remember that incident with the chicken? Well, the colonel remembers it too.'

The lesson, I guess, is that not all enemies wear a different uniform. **You will likely always have adversaries, and you won't always get your just reward.** Keep on trudging and try to let it go – don't still be telling the story eighty years later. (This might be a good time to say some lessons are harder to grasp than others; learn not to beat yourself up about that.)

By the time we approached the German border, reports of Nazi atrocities were widespread. Roosevelt, Churchill, and Stalin issued joint declarations promising that Nazi leaders would be held responsible for war crimes. I was surprised but not unhappy to be transferred to General Patton's Third Army HQ, which had received orders to set up a war crimes branch. My name had been forwarded from Washington. The Lt. Colonel who greeted me promptly said, 'Tell me, Corporal, what is a war crime?' My time had finally come! **Lives are pathways that don't run straight.** They twirl and climb and plunge and are littered with bumps along the way. When you get to a bit with a view you like, all of the diversions will have been worth the experience, however much you hated them at the time.

In due course, we received reports that Allied flyers who were shot down, and those who parachuted into German territory, were being systematically murdered on the ground, in violation of the laws and customs of war. So it was that the Allied Flyer cases came into being. I would get into a jeep and head to the scene of the crime to retrieve evidence for an investigation. It was grim work. The bodies would have been dumped into a river or a hole somewhere. Usually the person was dead, stripped; sometimes you could find the serial number in permanent ink on the inside lining of his pants. I had to arrange to dig them up. It was wintertime and the ground was hard, but I didn't dare use a pickax lest I hit a man in the head, and could not distinguish the injury from a stab wound or bullet hole. I'd tie a rope around one or two ankles and attach the rope to the back of my jeep and slowly try to extract the body, hoping that I got more than a foot. I was usually the only American on the scene, and the sole authority I had was a .45 caliber pistol on my hip. Later, I had the front of my vehicle painted in bold letters with the German words, 'IMMER ALLEIN', meaning 'always alone'.

When the war drew to an end, I went on the hunt for the biggest fish of all, Adolf Hitler, who was suspected to be hiding in his Eagle's Nest, an elegant hotel atop the Alps in Berchtesgaden. I borrowed a trailer from a chaplain with the anticipation that I might need more than a jeep to bring back any evidence that I might find. But the Eagle's Nest had already been bombed, and craters littered the winding road up to its majestic setting. I couldn't drag my trailer along, so I left it with some American soldiers guarding the road. The nest had been occupied by the 101st Airborne Division, and Hitler was nowhere to be found. I went immediately to the file cabinets and made a great discovery: the second drawer from the bottom made a very convenient toilet, and the 101st Airborne had used it frequently. Whatever those documents were, I wasn't taking them home.

We received reports that Hitler had committed

suicide in Berlin. I regret that I was never able to pay the Führer a surprise visit. When I arrived at the bunker the Russians had already dug a big hole, at least ten or fifteen feet square, into which they had deposited his ashes.

Back in the headquarters in Munich, I had to explain to the chaplain I'd borrowed the trailer from that I'd lost it. I said, 'Father, I've just come back from the field.'

He said, 'How did you do?' I said I'd lost my rifle, and he said, 'Don't worry about that, my son.' I said I lost the souvenirs I wanted to bring back for the others, too, and he said, 'Don't worry about that either, God will forgive you, my son.'

I said, 'But I also lost your trailer.'

Silence.

They tried to court-martial me for the loss of government property! I threw the papers in the garbage, of course.

5

On Principles

CHOOSE TO BE GOOD

It was during the Allied Flyer cases that we began to get reports to General Patton's headquarters that tank battalions had encountered people on the roads who looked like they were coming out of some sort of a work camp. The reports said they all looked like they were starving, and that they were dressed in rags and pajamas. They were, of course, the inmates fleeing the concentration camps that had been liberated.

I went to about ten camps, including Buchenwald, Mauthausen, Flossenbürg and Ebensee. The scenes of death and inhumanity were identical in all the camps. I remember it very, very vividly, and have difficulty describing it even now. You carry that with you for the rest of your life. The total chaos. The battle still somewhat raging. Bodies lying all over the ground, some dead, some wounded, begging, weak, pleading with their eyes for something. I've seen piles of skin

and bones piled up like cordwood, helpless skeletons
with diarrhea, dysentery, typhus, TB, and pneumo-
nia. I've seen people crawling through garbage like
rats, digging with their hands for a piece of bread or
a morsel to eat. I've seen the crematorium going with
bodies shoveled in, their ashes spread on the field like
fertilizer.

They were scenes of indescribable horror. It was as
if I had peered into hell. So I devised a system. I pre-
tended it didn't exist. Normally I'm a pretty rational
guy, but I would say to myself, 'It's not real, it's not
real, it's not real.' I would pretend it was part of a show
of some kind. What else could I do? I couldn't sit
down and start screaming and tearing my hair out, or
grab some German and beat him over the head with
a hammer. **There are things our brains weren't
made to compute, and at those times we must
trust that they know the best way to protect us.**
People who are grieving often say they need to go to
sleep at unusual times of the day; if your mind can't
handle the pain, it follows that it will need to switch
off more than usual. And so it went for me that in
order to get through the terror I was witnessing, I
imagined it was fictional.

I told myself to do my job. I would go into each
camp with the troops who were going in, or had

already been in there for a day or two. I would invariably do the following: I'd go to the commanding US officer and say, 'Look, I'm here on the orders of General Patton, we're carrying out a policy of the United States government. I want ten men immediately surrounding the office where the records are kept. Nobody goes in or out without my permission.' I acted like I was General Patton himself. I'd take possession of the *Schreibstube*, the camp office. You could always count on the Germans for their records; they were meticulous note-takers. I could see what had gone on in the camp. The list of inmates, their numbers when they were first sent to Auschwitz to be registered, which transport they were with and when the first transport arrived from Hungary, Romania, or Germany. Of course, most of them were already dead.

With that information I would go back to my typewriter and write up a report of what I had seen and who were the people responsible: who was in charge of the camp, how many people were killed, who the guards there had been. On that basis, we'd send out arrest orders to have them picked up. Do your job: seize the evidence and move on to the next camp. Move on. It was that attitude which kept me from going stark raving mad.

I distinctly remember meeting an inmate who

worked in the *Schreibstube* at Buchenwald, who I believe was a French national. 'I've been waiting for you,' he said. 'Come with me.'

He took a shovel and went to the perimeter of the camp, which was a barbed wire fence, and we dug up a box. We went back to the office and dusted it off. From it he took out a number of little booklets, which looked like passports. The SS carried the books, and every time they showed up for an evening meeting of the camp's social club, where they would drink and frolic, they had to present their booklet and get a stamp in there.

When the booklet was filled with fifty stamps, this inmate who worked in the office was told to dispose of the old one. But instead of destroying them, he hid them. He knew, in an act of faith, that there would be a day of reckoning. If he had been caught they would have killed him on the spot right there and then.

There are few situations where the majority of people will find themselves doing something while in fear for their life, so the lesson here is not to be brave like this man (although of course that would be a very fine thing). The lesson is that humans are capable of terrible things, but they are also capable of great things, however big, however small. **The world is full of good people who do good deeds;** sometimes just remembering that, and holding onto it, can be enough to rally us, inspire us and make us feel better about the history we are living through.

In real terms, this man's gift was a goldmine for me. These guys, the perpetrators and accomplices, were all going to tell me they hadn't been there, but I had the dates they showed up for the club, I had their number, I knew who they were. I immediately sent out arrest warrants, including to all the POW camps. The whole incident was an illustration of the courage of people who are facing death to do something by way of justice.

Often in the camps the remaining SS would be fleeing the scene. Most of the inmates were too sick or weak to move, but there were still a number of them who were in pretty good shape, who were up and about. In one camp I saw them catch one of the guards and begin to beat him. When he was semiconscious, they put him on a gurney and dragged him to the crematorium and put him in and began to cook him. They left him in there for a while, but not enough to kill him. They dragged him out again, beat him up again and put him back in again. They did that three or four times until he was sufficiently well baked and surely dead. I saw the whole thing, and I can still see it. But I thought gee whiz, if I try to stop these guys, they'll turn on me.

On my way between camps, I met some advance units of the Red Army, who took me into a celebration. One of the Russian soldiers asked me what I did in the American army, and I told him I was a war crimes investigator, seeking evidence of what the SS did. 'Don't you know what they did?' he asked. I said of course I did. 'So why are you asking them?' he said quizzically. 'Just shoot them.'

Vengeance is a horrible thing. Vengeance will follow murder. The French would take some of the girls who had been cohabiting with the German soldiers and put them in the town square and shave the hair off their head while the other civilians would spit on them or slap them in the face. When I witnessed that I would fire my gun into the air and say, 'Get away, she's under arrest.' I would put her in the jeep, drive her away and say, 'Now get out of here, go home.'

In my opening statement at Nuremberg I said, 'Vengeance is not our goal.' I knew what vengeance did; I saw it in action and believe me, it's horrible. My goal was to establish a rule of law which would protect everyone. It is a human thing to want vengeance, but we must struggle against it. **Don't become what you hate – if you do, you'll become someone else's**

enemy and the cycle will go on endlessly. The old adage to 'rise above' has value. Sure, everyone says it, but that's because it's true. This doesn't mean we shouldn't all be judged for our actions; it's just that's what justice is there for.

Of course, throughout the whole experience I was very mindful that I was Jewish, but I did not act any differently because I was raised in a Jewish household, nor did I distinguish the victims according to their religion. The only time I acted consciously along those lines was later at Nuremberg, when I didn't want my being Jewish to paint the trial as Jewish vengeance, so I gave my cross-examination of my lead defendant who killed 90,000 Jews to a friend of mine.

In the camps, the Jews were supposed to wear a Star of David, and the communists were supposed to wear a red star. But by the time I got there the uniforms were rags and unidentifiable. They were all human beings.

6

On Truth

Always Speak Yours, Even If No One's Listening

When I returned from Germany, I joined over ten million other American soldiers in looking for work. I sent job applications to wherever I could. The first question the big law firms would ask was, 'How many clients can you bring with you?' Unfortunately the only clients I knew and had were people with nothing but a tattoo on their arm.

I was having trouble finding work, when one day I got a telegram from the Pentagon saying they'd like to talk to me. So I went to Washington, where I was interviewed by Colonel Mickey Marcus, who was recruiting staff for military trials being planned by the army. There was an acute shortage of lawyers who knew anything about war crimes trials, and the army was desperate.

I wasn't thrilled at the prospect of returning to military command, and the tribunals left much to be desired, but then I was asked to go see a second colonel: Telford Taylor, and that turned out to be significant. Taylor said he'd been appointed by President Truman to be responsible for additional trials to be conducted by the United States government, designed to expose various facets of German life, to explain how it was that a country as civilized as Germany could perpetrate such horrible crimes. They were going to set this up as soon as the international military tribunals were over.

Taylor said he had checked my record and found me to be occasionally insubordinate. I said, 'I'm sorry, sir, that's incorrect. I'm not occasionally insubordinate, I'm usually insubordinate. I don't obey what's illegal or stupid.' I told him that luckily, I had also been checking up on his record, and knew that he wouldn't give me that kind of order.

He smiled and said, 'You go with me.'

The Nuremberg trials would cover the whole panorama of German society. Telford said we had a number of suspects who had already been imprisoned but not the evidence to convict them. So I was tasked with finding the evidence to put on twelve trials, which dealt specifically with branches of German government and society. First were the doctors who performed medical experiments on concentration camp victims; then we had the lawyers who perverted the law by convicting people for political purposes. We had the industrialists who provided the funds to build the camps so they would have slave labor; the diplomats who paved the way for Hitler's wars of aggression; the military, and the Stormtroopers themselves who did the actual killing. This was all planned, and I was supposed to procure the proof of guilt beyond reasonable doubt.

I set up headquarters in Berlin and put together a staff of about fifty people and assigned them to various arms of the government. It must have been the spring of 1947 when one of our diligent researchers, Frederic S. Burin, burst excitedly into my office and said he had found something. He handed me a collection of reports – marked top secret – which had been bound into a thick New York-style phone directory. The reports had been sent by the Gestapo office in Berlin to perhaps a hundred top officials of the Nazi regime. Many generals were on the distribution list, along with high-ranking leaders of the Third Reich.

The daily reports, called 'Reports of Events in the Soviet Union', were from a unit called *Einsatzgruppen*, which turned out to be an SS extermination squad, deliberately given a nondescript title in order to conceal what their job was. But their job was very simple: they had been organized by Göring and others to kill all the Jews in the Soviet Union and any surrounding countries in Europe.

The *Einsatzgruppen* were organized in four units ranging from 500 to 800 men each. The reports were a chronology of how many civilians those units had killed as part of Hitler's 'Total War'. When I passed the figure of one million, I stopped adding. It's common knowledge now that the Nazis purposely killed six million Jews and eleven million others, but learning that information for the very first time, from records that were in front of me, was incomprehensible.

Jews, Gypsies and those considered enemies of the Reich. The plan had been to have these units follow behind German lines as it crossed Europe, which they expected to capture very quickly, and kill them all. The *Einsatzgruppen* would line up entire villages in front of mass graves and gun them down. People were treated like vermin to be exterminated. It was methodical. It was direct human-on-human savagery. That was the program, and I had the report in my hands.

I booked the next plane to Nuremberg and said, 'General Taylor, you've got to put on another trial.' He said he couldn't, that the lawyers had all been assigned and the budget had already been set. It was then that I blew my cool and said, 'We can't let these murderers go!'

I said we had in our hands clear-cut evidence of genocide on a massive scale, distributed to all the higher echelons of the Nazi hierarchy, all of whom said they didn't know anything about it. Had they forgotten how to read?

In desperation, I suggested that if no one else was available I could do the job myself. Telford asked if I could handle it in addition to my other responsibilities, and I assured him that I could. 'Okay,' he finally said. 'You do it.'

And so it came to pass that little Benny boy from Transylvania became the chief prosecutor of the biggest murder trial in human history. I was twenty-seven years old when the case opened in the main courtroom of the partially restored Palace of Justice. It was my first-ever case.

There were three thousand members of the *Einsatzgruppen* who spent practically every day on the Eastern Front murdering innocent men, women, and children. Since the days when merchant vessels first crossed the seven seas, it has been established law that he who sails on a pirate ship, knowing the purpose of the vessel, shall when apprehended walk the plank. But there was no way we could gently shove thousands of men into the sea.

So I decided the number that could be tried was limited to the number of seats in the dock: twenty-two. I selected my defendants on the basis of three important characteristics: whether we had them in custody, their rank, and their education. I decided that no enlisted men would be prosecuted – I wanted only the highest-ranking and most educated. If they didn't have at least one doctorate degree, they didn't qualify. I had one guy, Rasch, who was Doctor Doctor. He had two doctorate degrees; I'd never even heard of that before.

We had to get ready for trial. We had the defendants and the documents. They had time to select their own counsel. Then comes the problem – what do I charge them with, and what do I recommend for punishment? Do I charge them with traditional war crimes, which had been prohibited by Hague conventions a hundred years earlier? I also charged them with genocide, because I knew the man who coined the term – a Polish refugee lawyer named Rafael Lemkin, who fled from his homeland after his entire family had been murdered by the Nazis, and who, like the ancient mariner of Coleridge's poem, collared anyone he could to tell them the story of how his family had been destroyed by Germans. I also charged the defendants with mass murder and crimes against humanity. I made the point that what happened, the scale on which it occurred, was a deliberate crime against humanity and should be prosecuted as such.

I was sitting on a Sunday morning in the courtroom by myself, writing out my opening statement, and I concluded very quickly that if the trial was to have any meaning it couldn't merely be about justice. I had selected just twenty-two out of three thousand mass murderers, and they were all equally guilty of either direct mass murder or conspiracy to assist in the murder of more than a million people. There was no way for the scales of justice to balance this. I knew that the trial had to stand for something more if it was going to have any significance. The people murdered were murdered simply because they didn't share the race, religion or ideology of their executioners. I needed to help deter the repetition of such horrors in the future, and lay the foundations for a more humane world. I needed to ask for the right of all people to be protected by law, so they can enjoy a life of peace and dignity.

This was just a selection of people to illustrate man's inhumanity to man: the ability of being inhumane, as all these educated, high-ranking Germans were. If you believe that another group is a threat to you because they have it in their blood to kill you, which was the Nazi doctrine as far as Jews were concerned, you logically act to exterminate them. But it's an inhumane consideration and a false argument, because it's not in the blood. We had to get a principle that will protect the people of the future against this type of action. I recognized that it could happen again, elsewhere.

My opening statement on the first day went as such: 'It is with sorrow and with hope that we here disclose the deliberate murder of over a million innocent men, women, and children.' I said the case we presented was a 'plea of humanity to law'. All the defendants without exception pleaded not guilty. There was no remorse or regret.

I'm frequently asked if I was nervous during the Nuremberg trials. I was an inexperienced young lawyer, facing Germany's mass killers, including six SS generals who would have shot me on sight. But I wasn't nervous, I was indignant. I didn't kill anybody – they did, and they knew I could prove it. I rested the prosecution's case in two days. I had all I had to say. 'Are you this guy? Is this your signature? Then you're damn lying.'

I concluded by saying, 'The defendants in the dock

were the cruel executioners whose terror wrote the blackest page in human history. Death was their tool and life their toy. If these men be immune, then law has lost its meaning and man must live in fear.' Little did it occur to me that the words would resonate and that we were indeed making legal history.

We moved on to 136 days of defense. The most interesting, and repulsive, argument in defense of genocide was put forward by the lead defendant, SS general Dr. Otto Ohlendorf. The reports stated that his unit, under his command, killed 90,000 Jews. He was asked if it was true, and he said he didn't know, because the men were inclined to exaggerate their body count. They wanted to show they killed more than they actually killed. Once the figure was corrected to 70,000, he was content.

Ohlendorf confirmed the Jews were killed simply because they were Jews. In the manner of a school-teacher, he explained that those with Gypsy blood were unreliable and might help the enemy, and there-fore had to be killed too. If the Jewish children learned their parents had been killed, they would grow up to become enemies of Germany, so they too had to be killed. He was interested in long-range security for his country, wasn't that clear?

Another justification Ohlendorf gave for his actions was self-defense. 'But Germany wasn't being attacked by anybody,' he was told. 'It attacked France, Belgium, Holland, Denmark.' 'Ah, yes,' he said, 'but Hitler knew, and Hitler had more information than I had. The Bolsheviks were going to attack us, therefore we decided we had better strike first. That's a legal pre-emptory strike.'

He introduced a big expert opinion from a criminal lawyer in Munich which said that's perfectly legitimate and not a crime. I did not think, decades later, at the age of ninety-nine, I would be hearing the President of the United States make the exact same argument at the United Nations General Assembly, when he threatened to 'destroy' North Korea if they threatened the US or any of its allies. There was no legal basis for a pre-emptory strike by Germany. We had three Nuremberg judges who held that it was not a lawful defense.

For Ohlendorf, war called for the suspension of humanitarian rules. He recalled the Allied bombing of Dresden and Hiroshima. His reasoning was a recipe for world catastrophe, and he was sentenced to death by hanging. Many others received a similar fate. Each time I heard that sentence, it was like a hammer blow that shocked my brain. I had never asked for the death penalty because I felt that it might trivialize the magnitude of the crimes by suggesting they could be settled by the execution of a handful. Others were sentenced to life imprisonment or long prison terms. When any of the Nuremberg trials was brought to a close, it was customary for the chief prosecutor to invite his staff to his home to celebrate the event. I think I was the only one who asked to be excused from my own party.

The lesson in this chapter might not, at first glance, seem like the most applicable to everyday life, but I believe it is, and it's one I must press upon you. People do not think what happened in Germany under Hitler could ever happen again, especially in their country. But it happened in Germany less than a hundred years ago, and no one thought it could have happened then either.

As I have said above, the defenses used by those on trial in Nuremberg are used today. Around the world, war crimes are still being committed. If we have not seen the crimes perpetrated by the Nazis matched by scale and organization elsewhere, we have still seen them since 1945. **The truth is a precious thing. Whatever yours is, don't take it for granted that people know it or remember it or can hear it. My** conclusion has been that war crimes are war crimes, no matter who perpetrates them; I have fought the powerful all my life to remind them of that fact and try to hold them accountable.

The defendants I had selected at Nuremberg were not ordinary criminals. All were men of intelligence and education. They had degrees in economics or law. One had been an opera singer, and another a Lutheran clergyman. All denied committing any crimes. My biggest lesson was that **war makes murderers out of otherwise decent people.** Ohlendorf was a good example. He was a handsome gentleman, the father of five children, who had earned a degree in economics. He was honest in his statements. His arguments were evil to me, but they were rational. I felt sorry for him, to tell the truth.

He was the only defendant who I ever talked to man to man, after he was sentenced to death. I went down to the prison where he was, right under the courthouse. I said I wanted to talk to him. I asked him in German if there was anything I could do for him. Some small favor, perhaps? A message I could relay to his family? He said that I would see that he was right: the Russians would have attacked, and the communists would take over. He began to repeat the arguments he'd made during the trial. The man had learned nothing and regretted nothing. I was a bit annoyed. I hadn't gone down there to hear that. I looked him in the eye, said gently in English, 'Goodbye, Mr. Ohlendorf,' and slammed the door in his face.

I was invited to attend the hanging. I declined.

7

On Love

THERE ARE MORE IMPORTANT THINGS THAN SAVING THE WORLD

I married my childhood sweetheart, Gertrude, and we had four children who brought us joy as well as grief. Gertrude and I met when I was still in high school. She was my stepmother's niece, and had moved to America from Hungary as a teenager with no knowledge of English, with no money and with no qualifications. At that point I didn't have much time or inclination for romance. 'Goils' were not in my repertoire, and the new girl in the neighborhood did not impress me much. I said she looked like a greenhorn. She called me a 'silly kid'.

In those days my older sister dominated me quite a bit, and was in charge when my mother was working. We had a fight one day because she told me to do something I didn't want to do. My mom said, 'You have to listen to her because she's your older sister. If you don't you'll have to leave home.'

So I said okay, I put my key on the table and left and went to my father's. I was fifteen or sixteen. My mother was shocked, and came to see me at my father's. Because I always treated my mother with respect, we discussed the situation in quiet detail. Gertrude, then living in the next room, overheard our conversation. She was touched by my gentle and persuasive reasoning, and soon came to realize that I wasn't just a silly kid. And I soon came to be impressed by her language skills, knowledge, and determination to go to night school to complete her education. The 'green' took on a rosy hue, and I began to notice that actually, she was very pretty.

So we began to take long walks, hand in hand, and became close friends. Then we started dating. I don't recall ever telling her that I liked her. I didn't need to; it was a gradual and mutual realization. One day it just happened. If I told you I remember our first kiss I'd be lying, but there were many kisses, many of them memorable.

Since neither of us had any money, our favorite pastime was going to Cooper Union to listen to lectures, a free and enlightening activity. The subway fare was only five cents, and we would often 'go Dutch' and share the costs. Sometimes I'd invite her to a hot chocolate at Stubies Ice Cream parlor on Tremont Avenue, or the Bronx Zoo to look at monkeys and sit on a bench to watch the sun set. My favorite singer back then was Bing Crosby, and I would serenade her with his songs, especially 'I'll Be Home For Christmas'. I could sing; as a singer she was pretty bad.

Gertie worked all day sewing in a clothing factory and all night in school. She was a bright student, eager to pursue a career in social work. We found we had much in common.

But I had decided I couldn't get married until I could support a family, because I had seen families breaking up due to a lack of funds. Gertrude and I discussed it at a very early age. I said I'd go to law school. I didn't know that a war would break out, and when it did, I told her that if she found somebody else, she shouldn't consider herself bound to me. But she waited patiently. Throughout the war, I was consoled by letters and photos from my 'pinup girl'. She kept all the letters I sent her in a shoebox and they were included in the archives I later donated to the US Holocaust Memorial Museum. They became 'national treasures'. **I would encourage all young lovers, even in this modern age, to write letters, cards or notes to one another** – they will be national treasures to you, especially in the future. It's important to let the ones we care about know how dear they are to us.

When I was offered the job in Nuremberg, I called Gertie from Washington and said how would you like to go to Europe for a honeymoon? She said, 'I'd love to.' I said, 'You've got it.' That's how I proposed. We got married, and then I left within a matter of weeks.

At the time, except for a few of the highest-ranking people, no wives were allowed to accompany their husbands overseas. As soon as I sailed, Gertrude applied for a job as a secretary in the war department in Nuremberg, but when it was discovered her husband was stationed in Germany, her employment was canceled. My wife remained stranded in New York, while I went to Berlin and set up offices to collect evidence for Nuremberg, and had to live in a bachelor quarters with a few other guys.

When army regulations finally changed, and dependents could be reunited with loved ones overseas, Gertrude was on the first army transport of wives scheduled to sail from New York to Germany. But before the ship could leave the port it broke down, and departure was delayed for a week. No sooner had they set out to sea again than fire broke out on board. They eventually reached harbor in September 1946.

Frustratingly, men weren't allowed to go down to the harbor to meet their wives. So I did what was within my power, and arranged to have a warrant issued for her arrest, which I intended to serve on her personally as soon as her ship docked. When I arrived at the dock, the guard asked if I had permission to be there. I said I was there to pick up a war crimes suspect, and got through.

At that point, the ship was tethered to the dock. As I approached it, the women hanging over the railings were screaming, 'There's Benny! That's Benny!'

Gertrude, of course, had explained to them that 'Benny will be here', no matter the obstacles in the way.

I went up the gangplank looking for her. I finally found her, whereupon we embraced and kissed. The captain was outraged. 'Who's that man,' he said, 'how'd he get here? Get him off my boat!'

I showed him my pass, and he said it wasn't worth the paper it was written on. War crimes prosecutors don't usually start embracing the witness! They picked me up and carried me off the boat. As I sat on the pier the women threw messages at me to call their husbands to let them know they'd arrived. I called them all up.

Gertrude followed me to Berlin, where she was

hired by the army because of her knowledge of German. I was using German researchers to go through the archives, so she ended up working for me. We occupied a house in a good neighborhood. It was a fun time.

We spent many happy evenings watching performances by Soviet opera and ballet stars on the stages of Berlin that we could never have afforded in New York. From time to time, Gertrude would interrupt my hectic schedule to remind me that we were supposed to be on our honeymoon. And she was right. **Be understanding and supportive of the obligations of your partner, but you can and should make time for one another, too.**

For our vacations, everything under communist control was off limits, but we did a pretty good job of seeing the rest of Europe. We went to recreational centers in the Bavarian Alps, as well as to Switzerland and Milan, where we stopped off at its famous opera house, and the gas station where Mussolini was left hanging from the rafters by his heels. Don't let anyone tell you the Ferenczs weren't romantics.

During the early postwar years in Germany, Gertrude acquired for us a new Mercedes sedan of about 1938 vintage. One of our early goals was to pay our respects to the memory of those who had been killed in combat. We visited US military cemeteries and war monuments, and considered putting up a sign at every gate asking, 'Was this really necessary?'

She was the Bonnie to my Clyde. Once, driving from Merano to Munich, I failed to recognize that the Italian Alps stood between us and our destination. In a show of my courage and command, I declared it no problem and drove us into the yonder.

But it soon transpired that there was no way we could make the top of the ridge and that we were in a precarious position on a cliff edge. The weather was getting colder and the nearest town was twenty miles behind us. We would probably freeze to death if we tried to walk back, and there was no person in sight to ask for help.

Trembling, Gertrude got out of the car to act as my guide. I carefully edged the car away from the cliff, fearing the swing of the pendulum, and skidded further into a ditch.

My thoughts in that moment turned to another Hungarian boy from Budapest who I had studied as a teenager, a magician named Harry Weiss – who went by the name of Houdini. He escaped from locked boxes by concealing a small jack on his person. I recalled the Mercedes had a small jack, and I used it to move the car inch by inch back onto the road. You can call it hocus-pocus. I call it teamwork.

Here's a lesson: **even if it means you have to admit you can't do something, it's better to turn back if you find yourself on the wrong road.** A stubborn driver who continues in the wrong direction might take you over the cliff. This lesson can also be applied to arguments.

Another time, Gertrude and I barely escaped death by parachuting from a burning plane over the ruins of Berlin. In 1948, while we were waiting for the judges to decide one of the cases, myself, Telford, Telford's deputy, and our wives were returning to Nuremberg from Berlin on an old C-47 propeller aircraft with two engines. The weather was miserable. It was raining, windy, and visibility was poor. We climbed into our parachute harnesses, as was the required protocol for such flights; when Gertrude complained that the straps were too loose, I joked that she probably wouldn't fall out (another one of my bad jokes).

We had only been in the air for a few minutes when General Taylor noticed the right engine was spewing oil. Within moments the engine began to backfire and the pilot had to immediately shut it down. The aircraft fell fast, and the captain yelled, 'Everybody out!' I grabbed Gertrude's hand and we rushed to the rear. There was a struggle to open the door due to the wind, and while I was trying to wrangle parts of my body through the gap, it suddenly blew wide open and I fell out into the clouds.

I yanked the ripcord of my parachute and slammed into the middle of a football field (I can't believe the US paratroopers turned me down, what wasted talent). As soon as I caught my breath I ran to a nearby house and called the control tower, who informed me the plane had just made an emergency landing. But an American woman had jumped off the plane before it landed. I asked for a description, and was told she was wearing a checkered jacket. 'That's my wife,' I screamed in German.

When I eventually got to Gertrude, she was disheveled and had suffered some cuts and scratches. When she saw me she burst into hysterical tears, having concluded that I had died when I fell from the plane. But she had followed me out anyway.

The next day I went back to retrieve my parachute. Though it was in Russian-held territory, I explained that it was the property of the US government. It later became a favored tent when we celebrated family parties in our garden back home.

*

Gertrude and I started having babies when we were in Nuremberg. We had four kids in five years. I wanted twelve – I figured it was cheaper by the dozen – but the doctor said if you want twelve you better get two more wives. We had our first daughter, Carol (who later changed her name to Keri), when I was twenty-nine. Shortly thereafter we had our next daughter, Robin Eve, our son Donald, and our last, Nina Dale.

I was thrilled to be a father. Life with the kids was a delight. We lived in a happy home. But that's not to suggest there was a shortage of problems. During one period, Gertie and I went to a psychiatrist for guidance, when the children were in their teens and out of control. He said you have to wait until they settle down and it's going to be okay, they have good parents, a good home, a good upbringing. **Remember this: adolescence is a time of temporary insanity.** We all did crazy things.

Gertrude handled the children's situations better than I did. Perhaps it was because as the head of the family I felt I had a special duty to try and help them avoid any hazards. After a full term at a boarding school in England, for example, my eldest daughters returned home because their mother, who was never enthusiastic about the idea, wanted them close. The girls, annoyed about the interruption of their holiday abroad, announced they were going to run away from home. Gertrude bought them each a knapsack, gave them some money, insisted they tell our family doctor where they were going, and warned them never to hitchhike. The next night she woke me to tell me our girls were running away. Keri, sixteen, had rigged a rope from her bedroom window over the roof so as to make a clandestine exit, and Robin, fifteen, just walked out the front door. A day later, our Goldilockses were picked up by some cops while hitchhiking in the area of Laurel, Maryland, and promptly escorted to a nearby children's detention center. We were much relieved.

I called up the judge and explained that I was a lawyer, and the father of the two young girls, and wanted to ask him for a favor. I asked him how long he could legally hold our daughters. 'We're not running a hotel,' he said. I apologized and said I would gladly reimburse the state for any expenses, but I feared that if our girls were released promptly, they would run away again just as promptly. The judge held them for ten days, during which their mother made several failed attempts to bail them out. But they never ran away again.

*

After I wound up all of the Nuremberg proceedings, I was approached by Jewish organizations that wanted me to stay and set up restitution programs. We only returned to America when my eldest was reaching school age because I didn't want the children to start school in Germany. At home, I once again struggled to find work. The big law firms said, 'Great, if we've ever got to hang a Nazi, we'll call you.'

So I began to take typical New York cases, like if someone fell down the subway and broke a leg, before setting up a law firm with my old buddy, colleague and plane crash survivor, General Telford Taylor. I became known as the lawyer who took on hopeless cases on a contingent fee – free speech cases, McCarthyism cases, and so on. I invested my money wisely and carefully and, from having been a poor boy, got to be a relatively rich one. It meant I could give it all away to good causes, and I continue to do so.

Meanwhile, as soon as the children were old enough to be left with a babysitter, Gertrude went back to school and got her degree aged forty-five. I went with all the kids to her graduation ceremony. Her report cards were always better than those of her children. She took further advanced education courses at night, received a master's degree in health education, and was eventually qualified to teach. It didn't take her long to get a new job in academia.

Unfortunately her first teaching job would be her last. She was employed by a rough high school where classroom doors often had to be kept locked. It was a grueling and frightening assignment. Even her requests that class sizes be cut in half were rejected until after she left. Together, we agreed that she should find a safer job, whereupon Gertrude volunteered to work for Planned Parenthood. There she encountered young girls, some of them rape victims, who came in for counseling and pregnancy advice. Afraid to talk to their own parents, doctor or minister, they were desperate for help. During the several years that she worked there, unpaid, Gertrude never tried to dictate what any person should do, she just set out the options. But I know it affected her a lot.

We carried on like that. Toward the later years of our life together, we would escape from the cold winters of our home in New Rochelle, New York to a small condominium apartment hideaway in Delray Beach, Florida. That's where I am now, and where my children come to visit me. My relationship with them is good. My son became a lawyer and has been working with me on world peace problems.

They're all college-educated professionals, all of them retired now.

Gertrude died on September 14th, 2019. I have a picture of her on her dying bed. In other pictures she looks like a movie actress. **But she was also beautiful from within, which was more important.** I appreciated her very much. We were married seventy-four years without a quarrel, and we'd been courting each other for ten years before that. I was very lucky. I was with her when she died, and held her hand all night long. I miss her very much.

I can't tell you what I liked best about her because I liked everything about her. She was kind, intelligent, decent, undemanding, tolerant. **Any difference of opinion was bridged because we respected each other's opinions.**

She was very patient, a good mother and a good wife. She always believed in what I was doing and tolerated my absences. All my books were dedicated to her, because I read all the drafts to her, and she would have her own suggestions and comments.

Ours was a real partnership. She was a constant companion in all of my work, sharing its problems and aspirations. Her patience and understanding were vital supports for all of my efforts to create a more peaceful world. The adage rings true, that behind every good man there is a good woman. The fact that we both came from similar backgrounds, faced similar hardships, shared similar values and goals, and were equally determined to make the world a better place, ensured a bond that lasted decades.

Winning her affections was my most important victory.

8

On Stamina

PUSH THE ROCK A LITTLE FURTHER UP THE HILL

I survived the war by damn good luck. I was short and therefore had bullets going over my head. **There's always a positive to be found from your shortcomings.** I rose from the rank of private, to colonel, to the civilian equivalent of brigadier general, which is not an inconsequential role. The army was not my preferred career, but through working hard and being useful I made something of myself in it, and if I hadn't gone into it, my life might have looked very different. Sometimes we are presented with ladders we don't want to climb – but that doesn't mean you can't climb them, and it doesn't mean you'll hate the view as you go. **Don't reject the situation in front of you because it isn't perfect, or your dream;** try your hardest, do your best, and you might find it is more rewarding than you first thought.

*

Nuremberg wasn't the end of the law's ability to help deal with the fallout from the war, and what came next would take many years. In my first year of Harvard law school – in the class of Torts – I learned something that anybody with a heart and independent mind would recognize. **If you do a wrongful injury to someone, you have an obligation to compensate them and make good for the harm.** Now it was time to test that principle on the biggest scale.

It had never happened in human history that the defeated nation in war paid compensation to the individual victims who suffered as a consequence of their illegal act, but I felt it was time that they did. Using that simple principle of tort law, I said, well, how do we go about getting compensation for what happened in the concentration camps?

After the war, the new countries of West Germany and East Germany had to come to terms with their immediate past. Not an easy task. The Chancellor of West Germany from 1949 to 1963 was Konrad Adenauer, a devoted Catholic and an anti-Nazi. In 1951, he made a public speech in which he acknowledged that terrible crimes had been committed against the Jewish people, and that there was an obligation on the part of Germany to try to make amends.

Based on that speech, the Chairman of the World

Jewish Congress, Nahum Goldmann, convened a conference to consider the Jewish claims against Germany. It was called 'The Conference on Jewish Material Claims Against Germany'. I was there. It took place in a hotel in New York. I had already been appointed under military government law to recover unclaimed Jewish property for individual victims, so I was considered an expert. The chairman invited other leading Jewish charitable organizations to attend that conference to begin discussing how we should respond to Adenauer's indication that something should be done.

I remember the doors to the conference were forced open by a group of young Jewish people who protested even discussing the question of compensation. Their attitude was, 'What, you're going to sit down and talk to the murderers of my parents about money? Have you no shame?' That same sentiment prevailed in the newly created state of Israel, which was rioting on this subject. But overall it was decided that the conference would meet with the West German government. We didn't take long to agree that we weren't going to ask for the valuation of human life, because you're not going to get into an argument whether Grandpa was worth more than Grandma. It's highly sensitive. We quickly agreed to ask for specific damages for the injury done. If you can compensate the individual, you should do that; if not, you have to do other things as well, such as pass laws to protect them in future, and create a set of standards for proper and improper behavior.

And so it was that, alongside a group of representatives of all the leading Jewish organizations in the world, I helped negotiate a treaty between the state of Israel – which didn't exist at the time the crimes occurred – the Claims Conference, and the new German government, which also didn't exist at the time the crimes occurred.

That was considered impossible. It was unprecedented in history. But West Germany gave billions to Israel, to the Claims Conference, and to other Nazi victims, Jews and non-Jews alike. It was not a straightforward or easy thing to do, but it is worth remembering the next time you have an idea you think is worth pursuing but everyone else tells you can never be. The greatest achievement of my career is what I did in connection with compensation for the survivors of Nazi persecution. **Everything is impossible until it's done.**

And so, by this point in my life, I had seen the fruition of many previously impossible things, and was determined to strive for another. **Seeing is believing.**

I hope my story might be of some inspiration to others, and it certainly can be. But one person's story is not enough to keep that belief burning, and a person who looks like you, sounds like you, is from the same place you come from, will likely be worth more to you. Seek out those people and their stories and fall back on them when your ambitions seem doubtful, or challenges have presented themselves. Struggling toward your hopes and dreams – whatever they may be – can make you feel like you're treading water out at sea. Building up a network of stories that prove others like you have done it before can help you see that there are foundations beneath you so tall, it's as if you're standing on the battlements of a castle.

And when you become a person who does the impossible, share your story widely so that others who look like you and sound like you can believe in themselves, too.

The presiding judge at Nuremberg, Michael Musmanno, felt strongly that 'where law exists a court will rise'. He saw an international criminal court as a means of diminishing future crimes against humanity and combating hatred and violence between ideologies. He expressed the hope that humankind, with a combination of intelligence and will, would be able to maintain a tribunal which would 'preserve the human race'. I adopted that hope, and retain it. And so I left the restitution program. I had a meeting with the Israeli adviser to the UN, Dr. Jacob Robinson, who also happened to be a respected friend, and told him I wanted to go work on the creation of a permanent international criminal court. Robinson said, 'Well, Ben, we hate to see you go, and you've taken on an impossible job, but it's worthwhile if you could do it.'

What happened in the Second World War might now seem like a movie, but it was real, and the battle we're faced with today is to stop it from happening again. I've written twelve volumes on how we can go about doing that, but in short, it starts and ends with a simple notion: changing the way people think about how they settle their disputes.

I thought I would try to do this because it was the right thing to do. I highly recommend using that as a guide to whether you should pursue something or not. **Don't think easy versus difficult. If it's a question of right versus wrong, then follow what's right.**

In the early 1970s I gave up the commercial practice of law to more fully devote myself to the cause of international justice. I wrote the books, I went to every meeting of the United Nations, I lobbied all the people, I wrote articles, gave lectures. I'd say,

'Look, we had a Nuremberg tribunal after the Second World War. Are you going to let it go and not create more tribunals? Are you going to throw that in the garbage?'

The International Criminal Court finally became reachable in Rome in 1998. I made an opening statement at the United Nations General Assembly conference for the establishment of the court, which was attended by 166 member states. I'd been nagging for so long. I said the place is here and the time is now. I said I have come to speak for those who cannot speak: the victims.

In the fall of 2000, toward the end of the Clinton administration, the deadline for signing the Rome statute was drawing close. One day I had a call from Robert McNamara, who had been the US Secretary of Defense from 1961 to 1968 during the war in Vietnam. He said, I want you to write an op-ed piece for *The New York Times* which both of us can sign calling on the US to sign on to the ICC. McNamara was the architect of the US military response in Vietnam. I said to him, 'Mr. Secretary, do you realize that if we had such a court, you might be one of the first defendants?' He said he was aware, and if he had known his actions were illegal he would not have pursued them. So I drafted the letter.

We must have been a powerful combination, because Clinton finally decided to sign the treaty. It was one of the last official acts of his presidency.

But unfortunately, his successor George W. Bush said we were no longer going to perform our obligation as a signatory state, and that's the political process. In July 2002, the ICC was established after the Rome statute was ratified by sixty countries. The United States was not one of them.

Although I've never had an official position (which is great: it means that nobody pays me, and so no one can fire me), I acquired a UN pass as a representative of a nongovernmental organization. I sat through at least a hundred meetings, listening to at least a thousand diplomats saying they couldn't define aggression, which was pure unadulterated baloney. They nitpicked the hell out of every proposed definition to find excuses to vote against it. One of the greatest difficulties was the US policy to oppose any permanent international court. Any country that submitted a case to the court would have their aid cut off. **The powerful will always be afraid of anyone trying to curb their power.**

But while America was the biggest opponent of that court, the biggest proponent was the most respected jurist in America, Justice Robert Jackson, Chief

Prosecutor for the United States at the International Military Tribunal at Nuremberg. This division of opinion exists even today. Most proposed changes in life – however big, however small – cause opposition. **People don't like change and can feel threatened by it.** Even when the thing you're saying sounds so obvious to you that your opponents' argument against it sounds akin to 'the grass is pink and the sky is yellow', opponents will still come. **Accept that fact now and try not to waste your energy on being angry when it happens; save it instead for whatever it is you're trying to do.**

While those in the current US administration will say, 'What court? It doesn't exist,' and the President, if he knows anything about it, will heed the words of his advisers, which is invariably to go back to killing as usual, I've had contact with people in the White House who are sympathetic to what I'm trying to do. Killing is not and will never be my approach – and I'm a combat soldier with five battle stars – and there are plenty of people who agree with me. As sure as you can be of opponents, there will also be people who think like you. **Find them, befriend them, get them to support you, support each other.**

In the late 2000s, the ICC's chief prosecutor, Luis Moreno Ocampo of Argentina, called me up and said,

'Ben, we're going to get to the closing of our first case, and we'd like you to do the closing remarks of the prosecution.' He was trying to connect Nuremberg to their first trial. It was a case against Congolese warlord Thomas Lubanga Dyilo, for recruiting child soldiers. He was convicted, and as far as I know he's still in jail. It was a small victory, a step forward in the attempt to prove you can't get away with that kind of massive crime without somebody putting you on trial. While it hasn't been without its faults and difficulties – call them growing pains – I hope the mere fact of the court's creation provides encouragement if you've been trying to get something off the ground for a few years or a few decades. **Just because it hasn't happened yet doesn't mean it won't happen. Don't expect perfection.**

We can't continue settling disputes by the current system, which is if one head of state doesn't agree with another head of state, they take young people from country A and send them out to kill young people in country B, who they don't even know and who probably never did them any harm. They keep killing each other until they're tired. Then they pause and they each declare victory, and then they start again. In another letter recently published in *The New*

York Times, I wrote about the US administration's announcement that, on the orders of the President, the US had 'taken out' an important military leader of a country with which we were not at war. I said such immoral action was a clear violation of national and international law, and the public was entitled to know the truth. I said we were in mortal danger unless we changed the hearts and minds of those who seem to prefer war to law. I refer you to Chapter 6 (On Truth): even when it feels no one is listening to your truth, you owe it to yourself and your conscience to speak it.

The main causes of war as I've studied them are threefold. The first is religion – people are willing to kill and die if they feel their god is being threatened. The second is nationalism – people are willing to kill and die if they feel their nation is being threatened. And the third cause is economic circumstances – if the wives and children can't be fed, they're willing to kill and die.

Ever since little David took down big Goliath, we've thought throwing rocks was a great thing to do. We have failed to recognize that you cannot kill an ideology with a gun. We think that if we go in and kill half of the enemy, then we're going to be victorious. That's idiotic thinking. And it's thinking which prevails today. There are dozens of countries right now out killing each other. Sometimes, like in Rwanda, you have people of the same creed and color, just with different variations in their religion, out slaughtering each other.

You cannot solve your problems by killing innocent people – they aren't the ones pulling the strings. Especially as, in the cyberspace age, the next war will be the last war. It will be the end of this planet. We must all condemn war, beginning at the earliest possible age. How can we do it? One word: slowly.

When I embarked on my crusade to create an international criminal court, I was perfectly aware that I was not likely to see it working perfectly in my lifetime. It takes longer than one lifetime to reverse something that's been glorified for years. But just the awareness that I could make an improvement, that I could push the rock a little further up the hill, was enough for me. There are three lessons I hope you'll take from this. One: something can be worth doing even if you're not around to see the end result or reap the rewards. It is a noble goal to want to do something that other people will benefit from, and it should be natural to want that for our successors. I don't just mean after you leave this life, I mean after you leave a job, or a governing body, or a school. **Act in the interests of the people who will inherit what**

you've done. Two: no man is an island. You cannot do it all. **Teams, communities, friends are key to our ongoing, and hopefully everlasting, successes.** And three: don't be distracted by speed. Remember the Tortoise and the Hare fable. **Not everything good can be achieved quickly and being fast doesn't guarantee success.** Quests for change don't exhaust me. Don't let whatever you care about changing exhaust you either if you feel the reward is worth it. The hope of changing people's minds about war has kept me going for almost seventy-five years.

How long change takes depends on how long the thing you're changing has been in place. It was always going to be difficult to turn around in one human lifetime something which has been glorified for centuries. You may not have noticed, so embedded in our culture is it, but we still glorify war – with the parades, and the flags flying, and the soldiers marching. I never go to the 4th July celebrations. The rocket glare, the bombs bursting in the air while everybody cheers, is for me a horrible thing, because I've lived through it and I've seen it – the bombs killing innocent people. What the hell are you celebrating? Good guys and bad guys? Adolf Hitler separated the world into good and bad. He was a guy who said to his country, 'We are the greatest.' *Deutschland über alles*. He believed that.

Where is he now? The Nazis killed millions, and what did that amount to? The current German government is now very much along my lines. The West German government gave me – once the enemy – their highest civilian award. I'm the guy that killed some of their heroes and jammed a compensation program down their throat.

Leaders and their peoples who say their country is the greatest, or who *want* their country to be the greatest, are small-minded. It's a great world, where all can exist peaceably together, or it's nothing. People who care only about making their nation great sound like kids fighting over their corner of a playground, and people who say a great unified world isn't possible have no vision, or else they benefit from the status quo.

I'm 100 years old now, and I'm very gratified with the amount of progress I've seen. I was told it would never happen, but it's happening, and we're seeing improvements. There are all kinds of laws to protect human rights everywhere. They're not very well enforced, but we have courts, including the ICC. Is it satisfactory? Of course not. Will it be satisfactory eventually? Of course it will. We've come further than I could have imagined. Every university in the world has courses on international law and human rights law. They didn't exist when I went to law school. The US constitution said women had no right to vote and couldn't own property. Now we have women and people of color running for and becoming President. Progress is real. **Don't worry about sentiments going up and down, what's important is the trend.**

Back to the ICC. At the moment, it's very difficult to get the court to move faster. Many suspects and their accomplices are in charge of the countries where serious crimes are being committed; they're not likely to let anybody in to investigate, which makes it hard to procure evidence or witnesses. The fact that we have a court is a great success. The fact that it's having difficulty with cases is unsurprising, but the people behind it are trying to do their best in difficult circumstances. The court is recognized, and people go out of their way to kill it because they're afraid of it. While we can't guarantee prosecution, at least we're holding forth the threat of prosecution, and we have a court which has authority in many cases already, so they're beginning to set a precedent of what is and isn't acceptable.

Many heads of state who commit war crimes are beginning to wonder if they're ever going to find themselves before a court. So far, the very powerful nations are not much concerned because they have their own nuclear weapons. But it's not so difficult going up against world leaders, nuclear weapons or no. Know why? Because I'm right. How can I go against a guy like the President? Easily. By speaking the truth. **Believe in what you're doing, and you can't be scared.**

Human beings should treat others as they would like to be treated, but we are failing at this every day. I see it in the news. They shouldn't kill others because they're of a different color, or deny them education, or hate that particular group, or take an infant away from the mother's breast and say 'your papers are not in order, we'll take care of the child, you get out of here', and chase them back to the country they fled in terror for their lives. You can't do that in a civilized world. Outwardly most people agree, but they have their caveats in practice. But you are either civilized, or you're not. There are no ifs or buts when it comes to being humane. The struggle to get the powerful to admit this continues.

Whatever you hope to achieve, don't worry if you don't win straight out, just make sure other people are listening that you can pass the baton to. I did a speech a couple of years back; the room was packed to the rafters with young people. Wild ovation. The assumption that the people cannot be aroused is not a correct one. There are so many distractions. Most young people don't have time to worry about politics. They worry about the next football game or dance, but you have to keep at it. The future belongs to them; when they figure that out, there's no stopping them.

But you big kids in the back, don't give up the ghost yet. Don't let anyone tell you your time's up. **Be passionate about something, keep that fire going, and you'll keep going too.** I have seen such horror that I can't rest. It's an obligation to my own conscience. I've got to keep trying to make this a more humane world for everyone. You might think I've become tired or cynical with age, but I've actually become more energized, and I can only hope this fire in me can be spread. **So be positive.** Whatever it is that bothers you, no matter how serious it may look, you're capable of overcoming it. I'm sure you've survived worse, and that's my guide, too.

And remember: if you can't reach an answer which is satisfactory, you can push the rock a little bit further up the hill. Increase the pressure. Write some more. Learn some more. Spread your message. Recruit more people. Never give up. One day we will see the mountaintop.

9

On the Future

Weather Eye On The Horizon, Hands On The Wheel

This book is so called because I'm in my 101st year, and so perhaps it will be my last. If I have anything to do with it, I will live for another 101 years, and these will be far from my 'parting words' (I have been known to be generous with my opinions, and I intend to carry on being so).

But as this is the final chapter of the book, for now at least, here are some parting words that I hope will help you go forth and live long, happy, healthy, and meaningful lives. I very much look forward to your own 100th birthday.

Pay attention to your health and fitness. I used to swim every day, but in case you're worried about not being a natural at exercise, it's worth noting that I wasn't always a natural in the water. During school, we had to pass a Red Cross life-saving test, and one of the requirements was to float motionless on the water for a couple of minutes. I told the swimming instructor that I couldn't float. He said, 'Nonsense, the human body is naturally buoyant,' and that he would prove it. He took me to the side of the pool, told me to take a deep breath, clasp my knees to my chest and roll over face down into the water. He assured me I would float like a cork. I did as I was told and, just as I had warned, sank head first to the bottom of the pool. He said I was the first person he'd ever met who wasn't buoyant, and I calmly informed him that it was because I had rocks in my head – something I'd heard often.

The instructor, sensing an opportunity, asked me if I liked bananas. I said yes. He explained that there was a water show at the end of the semester and that I could play an unforgettable role. All I had to do was jump into the pool with a banana, then sink to the bottom, where I would peel the fruit, stuff it into my mouth, blow out water, and rise back to the surface waving the peel at the audience. And I did that, to the glee of the amazed crowd. It was quite the show.

Years later, I was having lunch at a little bistro in Paris, and I noticed a guy at the next table kept looking at me. Finally he came up to me and said, 'Is your name Benny?'

Glad to have been recognized for my work, I said yes. He slapped me on the back and said, 'Boy, the last time I saw you, you were stark naked under eight feet of water eating a banana.'

These days I follow my own invented regime of exercises which takes me around twenty minutes each morning. I try to exercise all the muscles in my body as much as I can. The first thing I do when I wake up is stretch out in bed. I do bicycle pedals while on my back. Then I do twenty-five sit-ups. Then I get out of bed and go to the door, open it, check the weather, and do inhaling exercises to get rid of the stale air in my lungs. I inhale twenty-five times and exhale twenty-five times. At the same time, I bend halfway down, and then a quarter of the way down, while flapping my arms like a bird flying. The neighbors of course are convinced I'm crazy.

I put the radio on so I can hear whatever stupid news is happening, and do some knee bends. Then I lie down on the floor on my stomach and kick with my feet backward, like a jackass. Finally, I do my pushups. I used to do 100; I've reduced that to seventy-five now.

Smoking, drinking and heavy foods are bad for you, but you knew that already.

A good sleep is very important to clear the conscience. I sleep between eight to ten hours a day, and I'm lucky that I've never had trouble sleeping. I'm often asked how I would rest after witnessing the horrors of war, but the answer is simple: I was so tired I passed out.

Try. When I was being physically examined for acceptance into the army, the doctor asked me if I had any problems, and I told him I had excess acidity in my stomach, which meant I often had a bellyache if I ate the wrong foods. He said in the army I wouldn't be able to get the foods I needed, so he wasn't going to approve me. I was very disappointed. I said let me try it, you can always get rid of me later. I survived. Always give things a go; you're already better than you think.

Life's not perfect, and especially when we've seen horrors or hardship, it's hard to be truly happy at all times. But we can find contentment in the realities. I've had a full life, I'm in good health, I had a wonderful wife, I have four kids who are well educated and socially minded. They're not in hospital or jail. These are facts that make me a lucky boy. There are facts that make you lucky, too, if you look for them.

I'm a New Yorker and we're tough and special, but there's nowhere like Paris.

Read books to inspire you. I like nonfiction best, books about religion most. But my favorite book, believe it or not, was *War and Peace*. When the war was over, I was on leave in Switzerland and my outfit left unexpectedly. So I hitched a ride on a boat where nobody on the ship knew me. They constantly wanted to give me a dirty assignment. I would hide under the stairwell reading that book.

Have fire in your belly.

Don't follow trends, make your own. I have a very good caregiver these days, and I tell her I'm going to go out wearing one black shoe and one red shoe. She says, 'You can't do that.' I say, 'Why not? I just want to make the point that these are perfectly good shoes, why do they have to match?'

If I was a movie star who came out that way, then everybody would go out buying the same kind of red and black shoes mixed.

The future is unpredictable and best-laid plans go awry. Keep a weather eye on the horizon, but most importantly be present: your hands are needed on the wheel most of all and the future has a habit of taking care of itself.

Don't die with loads of cash in the bank. What good will it do there? Have enough for a rainy day, then give to charity if you can and share with your family.

Failure is a state of mind. Treat it like a hurdle on the way to success rather than a dead end. If you fall over one, pick yourself up and keep on going, and do what you can to make sure the same hurdle doesn't trip you up next time.

Never let anyone say they want to die for their country. That's stupid. You should want to live for your country.

Everyone should be considered innocent until proven guilty.

Never trust a politician. They're interested primarily in trying to get re-elected, and for that purpose they're really ambitious. I'm not saying everybody who holds a political position is corrupt. Some go down fighting, and do whatever they can do, wherever their particular offices may be. But many think primarily of themselves, and the public interest is further down the line. Routinely hold your politicians accountable for their actions, especially if you voted them in.

How do you mend a broken heart? It's like when I'm asked how do you get a peaceful world. There's a ten-volume answer for both, and also a one-word answer: slowly.

No matter how serious the situation, it's important to have fun. I have fun every day. As you may have guessed, I like to be funny.

Even Nuremberg was a great fun time. I got my reputation as a man who could create endless sources of beer at no cost. The OCCWC (Office of Chief Counsel for War Crimes) lawyers were lodged in a villa about ten miles from the court, euphemistically dubbed 'bachelor's quarters'. It would have been ideal except we weren't supplied with any food. The other five lawyers elected me to find a solution. I first phoned up the motor pool and ordered the corporal to send a jeep over. When they tried to play hardball I said how would you feel if the starvation of General Taylor's staff were on your head?

I took the jeep to the quartermaster's depot, where I filled out some forms to authorize distribution of food to a new mess hall. But one of the questions asked was the number of persons to be served. I, being an honest man, replied that there were six people. 'Sorry, buddy,' said the sergeant on duty. 'There has to be a minimum of twenty-five. I can't help you.'

I knew the sergeant would be going off duty in half an hour, so I thanked him, wished him well and departed. I drove around for half an hour and returned to greet the new guy on duty. When he came to the question of how many men were to be fed, I, being an honest man, replied, 'It varies, but give me the minimum and I'll let you know if I need more.' No problem. I was assured of sufficient supplies.

The beer ration had to be picked up directly from the local Nuremberg brewery. I acquired a Nazi command car, an oversized jeep that had been captured by the US Army.

I don't recall how many barrels of beer were authorized for consumption by twenty-five soldiers, but whatever it was, it meant six soldiers could have a hell of a time. The brewery was an enormous plant and there was no way I could pick up so much beer without help. I learned that the brewery delivered barrels in wagons to all the local bars. I located the one closest to our quarters and made a deal with the owner: I would instruct the brewery to drop off my kegs there, he would put the beer into bottles that would be kept on ice pending my pickup, and he could keep half for himself.

And so the Benny Beer Distribution System was born. Every night was a party night in Nuremberg. We were waiting for the trials to start, the terrible war was finally over and we were feeling victorious. There was a change in morals; there were no social patrols. Anyone who urgently needed a few cases of beer could call me up. Once I was convinced it was in the interest of my country to meet the demand, I phoned my partner at the local bar and told him to hand over a set of cases to anyone who would identify himself by the code words 'Benny sent me'.

I got the reputation of a man who performed miracles. My fame and popularity in Nuremberg wasn't based upon my prosecuting the biggest murderers in history in the shortest possible time, but on my mysterious ability to provide unlimited free beer to all the lawyers and their friends.

Be your own hero. I never had idols. I went to the Yankee Stadium and saw Babe Ruth hit a home run. Everybody got very excited about that. I didn't. So he can hit the ball harder than somebody else, so what? We're all trying to hit our own home runs.

Be comfortable. I always look like a bum; it's my normal attire. I call the tie, jacket and fancy pants my working clothes. If you see a television show where I look very respectable, know I'm usually sitting here in white socks, loose slacks and no tie.

Don't take yourself too seriously. I've been very lucky, to go from where I started out to where I am now. I'm very conscious of that, so I don't complain about little things. I don't make a big problem out of a small problem. Roll with the punches.

The best qualities a person can have are integrity, affection and tolerance. Never do anything you're ashamed of.

I'm looking at a picture on my desk of my wife and me. It's in a frame that says 'forever' on it. I carried that picture of us in my pocket all through the war. Carry your loved ones with you wherever you go, even if they're no longer here. Love is forever.

Acknowledgements

I would like to express my gratitude to Nadia Khomami, a journalist and reporter for the *Guardian*, for her time and effort in recording and transcribing the interviews which formed the basis of this book. I would also like to thank Emily Barrett, an editor at Little, Brown Book Group, for her helpful role in bringing this book to fruition and for having conceived the idea of my conveying life lessons to the general public in the format presented herein.

I would be remiss if I did not thank those of you reading this who share my interest in making it a more humane world under the rule of law, and to all of you I offer three words of encouragement: never give up!